GROW YOUR OWN
IN LANCASHIRE

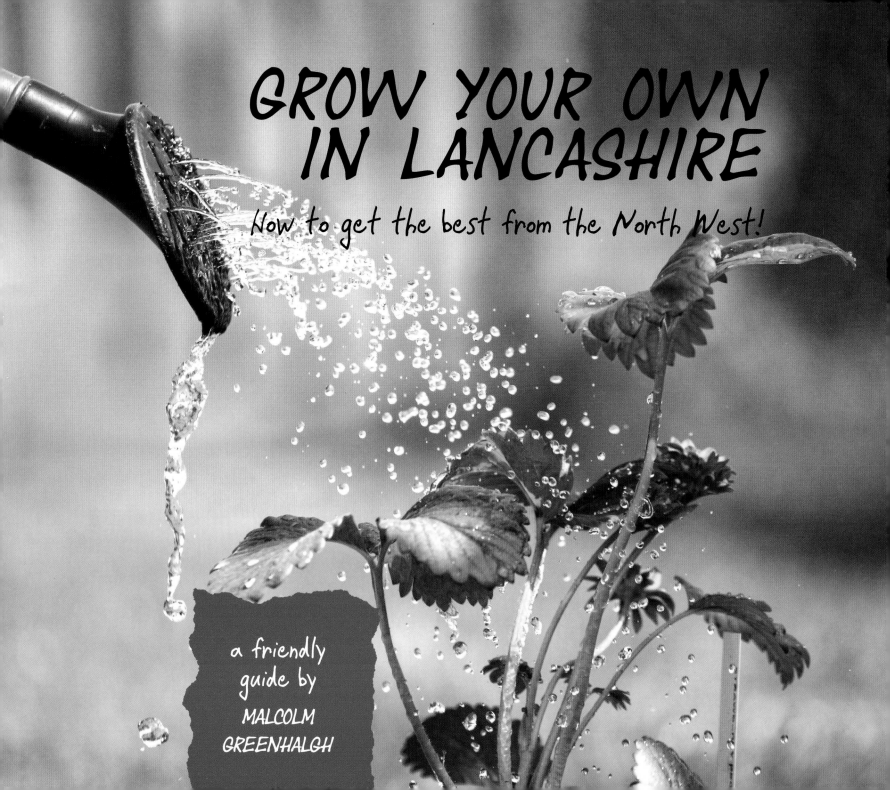

GROW YOUR OWN IN LANCASHIRE

How to get the best from the North West!

a friendly
guide by

MALCOLM
GREENHALGH

First published in 2014
by Palatine Books,
Carnegie House,
Chatsworth Road
Lancaster LA1 4SL
www.palatinebooks.com

British Library Cataloguing-in-Publication data
A catalogue record for this book is available from the British Library

ISBN 13: 978 1 874181 93 4

Designed and typeset by Carnegie Book Production
www.carnegiebookproduction.com

Printed and bound by 1010 International

Photos on pages 3, 39, 44 and 46 by kind permission of Karen Jackson,
thegardensmallholder.wordpress.com

Photo on pages 12-13 by kind permission of Jason Smalley,
jasonsmalley.co.uk

The Lancashire that this book covers is the old Palatine county, which includes parts of what are now Greater Manchester, Merseyside, Cumbria and Yorkshire. As with any gardening book, this one cannot claim to be comprehensive. It does cover the main issues and crops that are relevant to the North West, but is not intended as an expert plant guide. For that sort of detail you will need to consult additional appropriate and reliable sources of information.

CONTENTS

INTRODUCTION

GQT, Percy and Adam

I was born in Bolton at 31 Croston Street on 25 April 1946. The house had (and still has) a small, sunless, back yard. Thankfully we moved to Kirkham, again to a house with a flagged yard but at the edge of town and with two market gardens beyond the back gate. For the summer school holiday of 1956 I was paid five shillings per week for disbudding literally hundreds of chrysanthemums and tying new growth to the supporting canes. Taking the string twice round the cane, once round the stem, and then making a reef knot became automatic; I still do it without thinking.

When I was 12 we moved house to 173 Watling Street Road, Fulwood, to the north of Preston. This had a lovely long garden with a warm, sunny, southerly aspect, but was simply grass and a few old, gnarled apple trees. As far as I was concerned, this was ripe for cultivating and my parents, who were too busy, left me to it once they had purchased for me a new spade, fork, rake and trowel. My grandfather, then a semi-professional gardener in his retirement, gave me a razor-sharp hoe.

'Tha mun keep this 'andy and sharp,' he advised. 'Use it every day and if a weed appears, get it!'

Grandfather also instructed me in the art of compost making, and in the bottom corner of the garden I constructed two compost bins from old bits of wood, and gathered into them every bit of dead plant material, including peelings from the kitchen. A few months later he plunged his hands into the centre of the compost and pulled some out.

'Perfect. Just like best butter!' he declared.

I had never dug with a real spade before and, having felled three apple trees to open up a veg plot roughly twenty yards by ten, I found the digging over of the thick turf very difficult. Grandfather visited when I was part way through that laborious task. He took a file and sharpened the spade's edge. Now the spade cut through the turf and ground easily and made the double-digging easier. 'Keep th'oe and t'spade sharp wi' this file,' said my mentor, as he handed me *his* file as a present.

I learned a lot from my first garden. For instance, I planted some fruit trees and bushes, including a Cox's Orange Pippin. That yielded only small, hard fruit, illustrating to me for the first time that what grows well in the gardens of writers and broadcasters in the south and middle of England will not necessarily grow well up here in and around Lancashire.

Nevertheless, undeterred, in 1958 I became a keen fan of Grow Your Own (GYO), producing potatoes, cabbages, sprouts, beetroot, turnips, beans and peas, lettuces, as well as strawberries, blackcurrants and loganberries, but failing to produce edible carrots. For it was that year that I met carrot root fly for the first time. I purchased my seeds from a long-gone store on Lancaster

Road in Preston, and instead of buying onion sets I bought shallot sets instead. I had never heard of shallots, but their sets were bigger so I assumed that they would grow bigger than onions. You can imagine my surprise when my shallot sets simply produced lots of similar sized shallots and, not knowing what to do with them, my mother just pickled them. That was long before the days of TV chefs and haute cuisine!

My biggest three inspirations as a novice gardener were GQT, Percy and Adam. GQT was, and still is, Gardeners' Question Time and in, I think, 1959 or 1960 I went to a recording of the programme in Preston's Public Hall. On the panel were Prof. Alan Gemmell, Fred Loades from Lancaster and the wonderful Bill Sowerbutts from Ashton-under-Lyne. Two Lancastrians! Over fifty years later, in 2011, I was tickled pink to be briefly interviewed by the chairman Eric Robson on this memory and then be able to ask a question in a recording at Warrington. The panel was Bunny Guiness, Anne Swithinbank and Bob Flowerdew. GQT is still essential listening for me on Sunday afternoons.

Percy was Percy Thrower. On Friday evenings Percy appeared in Gardening Club on BBC TV (no BBC2 etc. then), in which he demonstrated gardening techniques in a pile of John Innes 3 compost that had been tipped onto the floor of the studios in Birmingham. Naïve by today's standards, perhaps, but perfect 'how to do it' without the unnecessary celeb hype and waffle that we get today on most gardening programmes!

Adam was Adam the Gardener, a cartoon character who appeared in the *Sunday Express* and whose weekly columns had been brought together for the whole year in one book. I followed Adam's advice to the letter; for instance, pruning my bush apples and blackcurrants when he did and as he did, and sowing my Savoy cabbages when he did and transplanting them when he did. In the summer of 1961 I even grew chicory and tried to force some the following winter. Alas, mine were tiny compared with the cartoon of Adam's!

Since then I have had several gardens and an allotment and, while I enjoy growing decorative plants like roses, azaleas, clematis and the like, my first love has always been fruit and veg and my last love lawns. Originally our present house in south Lancashire had a large lawn (30 yards long by up to 15 yards wide) at the side and two smaller lawns front and back. Now the front lawn is a rose bed and the side lawn is almost entirely fruit and veg (save for maincrop potatoes, it produces well over half the requirements of my wife and I). I also have a greenhouse for glasshouse crops on what was part of the back lawn and many containers dotted around the place.

Why do I work so hard on GYO? Because I love good food. And if you love good fresh food, grow your own.

Malcolm's grandfather Herbert (Bert) Haslam, in his gardening overall and boots, resting in Malcolm's first garden in Fulwood, Preston, in 1959.

Adam the Gardener.

OCTOBER   First Week

SIX GREAT REASONS . . .

1. You can eat it when it is much fresher than market or (even worse) supermarket produce. A cabbage, tomato or bowl of strawberries eaten within minutes of picking have more vitamins and minerals and far more flavour than produce a couple of days old.

2. You can choose varieties that taste much better than those grown commercially. You will not, for instance, find potatoes like the old Arran Pilot, tomatoes like Shirley, carrots like Rondo, or salsify, in the shops. So if you want to enjoy these wonderful varieties you have to grow them.

3. You can grow 'organically', by which I mean that you can grow without using the vast quantity of chemicals and pesticides used by commercial growers. You may also use 'organic' fertilisers.

4. GYO keeps you fit. Standing up, and bending down, and weeding with a hoe will burn up far more calories than sitting in an armchair and watching sport on TV!

5. GYO is educational, if not for you then for your children and grandchildren. I have known children who did not know that potatoes grew underground and I once met a woman from Liverpool who thought that sprouts grew on the soil like mini cabbages.

...TO GROW YOUR OWN!

6. GYO can be very sociable. Join your nearest gardeners' association. There you will meet more experienced gardeners who will be able to give useful advice. Some, like Newton-le-Willows Gardening Association, have monthly demonstrations by visiting experts, coach trips to shows, a website giving useful tips and a sales and information hut where you may buy seed and potting composts, canes, fertilisers etc. at prices lower than DIY stores and garden centres. They also have a half allotment set aside for educational purposes, to show people techniques and how to overcome problems they may face. Being a member of a gardening or allotment association is a very good idea, not least because when you have a problem, there will usually be some old hand who will know the solution.

A word to the wise: don't grow your own simply because you think it will be less expensive than buying fruit and veg. This may well be the case in the long run, but you will need to put in time and effort before you see a return on your investment. For example, this year my three blueberry bushes (which cost about £30 just over a year ago), planted in a mix of ericaceous compost and coarse sand (cost c.£15) had a great crop of about 5lbs of fruit. In the supermarket that weight of the fruit could be bought for about £25. Of course, mine was fresher, picked at 7.30 a.m. to go with our cereal, and tasted fabulous, but it will be another year before I am in profit.

PART
ONE

make the best of
what you've got!

GARDENING
IN THE
NORTH WEST

AS A NOVICE GARDENER IN THE 1950S it didn't take me long
to learn that I couldn't expect certain crops to thrive in the
particular climate and soils enjoyed by the North West. And
not long afterwards came the realisation that the information,
advice etc. on offer in books, magazines and on TV and radio
was somewhat skewed towards the south of the country.
So began my quest, partly by research but mostly through
experimentation, to identify those vegetable and fruit varieties
with which Lancastrian growers can succeed. You will find
many suggestions of same within these pages, but first a look
at what we all have to contend with in terms of the specific
characteristics of the region – and it's not all bad.

Collect lovely fresh rainwater where you can, even diverting it straight from your downspouts – as long as you can keep up with any torrents!

Rainfall

The late John Arlott once told his listeners, when rain stopped play in a Test Match at Old Trafford, 'Manchester is the only city in the world where they have lifeboat drill on the buses!' And it's true, generally Lancashire does have a wet climate compared with much of the rest of England, due to the prevailing south-westerly winds that bring warm moist air in from the Atlantic. As the air moves inland it rises as the land rises, cooling, and as it does so precipitation occurs.

As a rule of thumb, on the coast in places such as Southport, St Annes and Blackpool there is roughly 20 inches of rain per annum, similar to London and East Anglia. But for Manchester, Bolton and Blackburn the figure rises to 30 inches (an incredible 56.15 inches in 2012, the 'monsoon' year!), and in the hills east of Oldham and Burnley 40 inches of rain falls from the sky every year.

However, prolonged droughts do occur, and in some recent years they have dominated spring (in 2009 April–early July, in 2010 April–June, and in 2011 March–early May), with cool, dry easterly winds persisting for weeks on end. This is sowing and planting time, when surface soil moisture is very important. So when sowing seeds, water the seed bed thoroughly before and after sowing; and if the drought continues, water well at least weekly until the young plants are established. When planting out things like brassicas (cabbages etc.), potatoes and onion sets, water well after planting. With water-hungry plants like runner beans and courgettes, make sure that the soil

You will often see slender little creatures swimming in the butts. They are mosquito larvae. Keep the butts covered if you want to be mozzie-free.

has lots of water-holding compost/manure and is never allowed to dry out. And – vitally important – when planting rhubarb, fruit bushes and trees, water weekly from the time of planting to the end of September; even if it rains.

Butt water contains bacteria and should not be used to water seeds or young seedlings. Use tap water for that, except for ericaceous plants.

We are fortunate in that we rarely have hose-pipe bans in Lancashire (2010 was an exception, but within days the heavens opened and the ban was lifted), but we ought to be more aware of the need to conserve water. Most of our tap water comes from rivers, via reservoirs, and after a few weeks of drought our rivers run low, threatening aquatic wildlife. So, save water by getting some water butts.

I have butts that collect water from the roofs of the house and my two sheds. I also have five old plastic dustbins, and when the butts are full I transfer water into them. When the 2011 spring drought ended in early May, all were nearly empty. By 17 May they were all full.

Our tap water often contains lime, and lime will kill plants such as azaleas, rhododendrons and – especially – blueberries. We once went on holiday and a pal volunteered to water things while we were away, but he used tap water and when we returned our blueberry bushes were stone dead. So I sunk our old bath in the ground, filled it with a mix of ericaceous compost and sharp sand, and planted a couple of blueberry bushes in it. They only get watered with rain or butt water and they love it.

17

Temperature

Generally the region's climate is cool in summer, mild in winter, but the higher you are, the colder it usually gets. My daughter and her family live in a village in the hills above Oldham, at 1016 feet above sea level. We live at Lowton, 75 feet above sea level. On more than one occasion we have left home in winter in not too cold conditions to visit grandchildren who are sliding on the ice and sledging in snow. So the further inland the greater the chance of late frosts in spring and early frosts in autumn. The problem is even worse in steep-sided valleys, for there cold air flows down the hillsides creating 'frost hollows' as late as mid May and as early as September.

So while those of us who live on the low Lancashire plain can have new potato plants well above the ground by the end of April and harvest runner beans well into the autumn, at many inland sites they would be killed by late or early frosts. I have been told that at Bakewell, in the Wye Valley of Derbyshire, it is almost impossible in some years to grow runner beans because of the frost-hollow problem.

Of course we do all get severe winters occasionally, as in 2010–11. That, alas, killed my fig tree that had been growing outside for 12 years and in 2010 yielded 54 delicious fruits.

Soil

It is important to appreciate that soil type varies tremendously within any given area, as it does within the boundaries of the old county of Lancashire. The map on page 21 should tell you, if you don't know already, which soil type you are likely to have in your garden, so that you can look in the relevant section below to see how to work with what you've got.

Sandy

These are arguably the most difficult to work with and many coastal gardens have soil of this type. Southport, Birkdale, Ainsdale, Formby, Fairhaven and St Anne's, and parts of Blackpool's South Shore and Fleetwood, were built, mainly in the nineteenth and twentieth centuries, on flattened sand dunes. Although builders may have laid a few inches of top soil on the sand, if you dig deep enough, the sand is still there. I

was once taken into a large Southport garden well over a mile from the sea, where a bucket of water drained away as soon as it was poured on the ground. Similarly, the little patch of garden my mother cares for at Fairhaven is so sandy that most plants that grow well elsewhere struggle, unless she waters them daily.

Sandy soils associated with underlying red sandstone, can also be found in South Lancashire (e.g. around Newton-le-Willows).

If your garden is of this type and you want to grow fruit and vegetables, it is essential to add large quantities of organic matter every year – and I mean very large! In a sandy soil organic matter oxidises rapidly and disappears. Hard work, and probably expensive. The alternative is to grow everything in containers – and why not, I say.

Peaty

May be found in the gardens of houses built on the Lancashire and Cheshire mosslands, that flat, black-soiled land that stretches from the outskirts of Manchester almost to Liverpool, from Liverpool north to Southport, and from Southport to nearly Preston, inland of Blackpool, and from Pilling through Cockerham to Lancaster. 'Pilling Moss,' the saying goes, 'is, like God's Grace, boundless.' It is the mossland that makes West Lancashire one of the greatest producers of vegetables in Britain.

However, even most houses built on mosslands do not have a peaty garden, for the peat will usually have long gone, often leaving an underlying silt.

Silty

Widespread on the flatter, lowland parts of Lancashire and north Cheshire, silty soils appear in parts that were once mossland or saltmarsh. After the last Ice Age the lowlands were very wet, with lots of shallow pools and lakes and streams carrying silt into them. With the ice gone, the land dried up and forest clothed much of the countryside. But then the climate became wetter from about 500 BC and Sphagnum mosses colonised the waterlogged soil. Tree roots suffocated and the trees fell into growing peat. Remains of these trees, called 'bog oak', can be seen on field edges in West Lancashire or on display at Martin Mere wildfowl centre near Ormskirk. Sometimes the remains of humans, sacrificed to ancient gods, are found, such as Pete Marsh, from Lindow Moss, west of Wilmslow. Where the peat was later removed, naturally or by humans digging it for fuel, the silty soil was revealed. Many gardens and allotment sites around Manchester, Newton-le-Willows, St Helens, the edge of Liverpool, parts of the Fylde and around Morecambe and across the Bay in Furness, have silty soils. So too have gardens on reclaimed saltmarshes (as at Marshside and Banks, near Southport and around the Dee estuary) and on river floodplains (as in the Lune and Ribble valleys).

You can consider yourself lucky if your garden has a silt soil. It will not be prone to waterlogging, and will not dry out like a sandy soil. It is easy to dig, and you can get a great 'tilth' for seedbeds. It doesn't hold water as well as clay soils (below), so in droughts watering may be necessary, though this can be reduced by adding garden compost or well-rotted manure either by digging it in or as a mulch.

Clay

This is probably the commonest type. Here we often have a grey, sticky clay called 'gley', though sometimes there are bands of red clay (as at places like Hesketh Bank and Accrington, where it was used to make bricks). The soil in all my gardens over the years have been gley clay, located in Fulwood, Brockholes (east of Preston), Tarleton, Bolton and Lowton. I have learned that to get the best out of a clay soil you must work hard, at least initially. Double-dig (see page 22) and incorporate as much organic matter as you can in there. But after the first double-digging, have a no-tread policy and the earthworms will do most of the hard work for you. A well worked clay soil holds moisture and plant nutrients better than any other soil and produces excellent crops.

Loam

A soil that contains a mix of particle sizes ranging from sand to clay is perfect soil, for it drains well enough not to become waterlogged after heavy rain but is slow in drying out. Alas, I have had no experience of such a soil, unlike the fortunate growers in the west of the county.

Soil pH

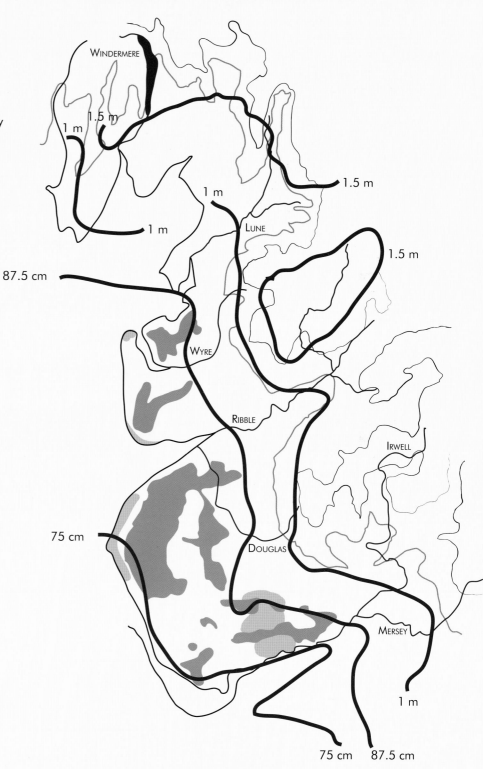

pH is a measure of acidity, pH1 being very acidic (it will burn the skin), pH14 very alkaline (it too will burn) and pH7 neutral. Note that a change of one unit of pH is a factor of ten; so pH6 is ten times more acid than pH7, pH8 ten times more alkaline than pH7, and thus pH6 is 100 times more acid than pH8. Generally we should be seeking a soil pH of 6–7.5 for our vegetable and fruit growing, so because Lancashire soils tend to be on the acidic side of this (pH5.5–6.5) we usually need to raise the pH by adding lime or ground limestone. This even applies to soil overlying limestone (as in parts of the Lune and Ribble/ Hodder valleys, around Carnforth and Silverdale, and in what is now called South Cumbria – the Furness/Cartmel areas) for rain and other watering carry away lime from the surface layer of soil. So buy a soil pH testing kit: they are very easy to use. I usually lime two years in four, before planting brassicas (lime helps also prevent that horrid disease of things like cabbages and sprouts, club root) and before planting peas and beans (that do like a soil pH on the slightly alkaline side of neutral). Beware of adding lime to the soil where blueberries are growing.

One of my no-tread beds, with compost waiting to be spread.

Double-digging & no-tread beds

This hard work will help soil structure, especially that of clay soils, to improve over successive years. Mark out the bed you are going to dig for the first time – I would suggest that beds be just wide enough for you to reach out into the middle easily from a path on either side. My own vegetable beds are about four feet (about 1.2 m) wide. From one end, remove all the soil one-spade deep in a band about 12–18 inches (30–45 cm) wide. Take that soil to beyond the far end of the bed in a wheelbarrow. Now dig down another spade's depth, turning that bottom spit over. Sprinkle a good layer of organic material (rotted cow muck, spent mushroom compost, garden compost – anything you can get your hands on, even shredded wet newspaper and cardboard) and fork that into the bottom spit. Now dig the next 12–18 inch-wide band to one spade's depth, but this time spade it onto the first band; as you do this, mix in more organic material if you can. Then dig the next spit down, put in lots more organic material, fork it in and continue double-digging strips. When you get to the last strip, fill it up with the top spit with the soil from the first strip that is waiting for you there.

It is important to remove ALL weeds in this digging, keeping a special look out for the underground stems of things like creeping thistle, couch grass and so on.

Voluntary diggers, who do it freely: earthworms. The more of them the better!

You will never stand on this kind of 'no-tread' bed ever again, for sowing, planting and harvesting are all carried out from the paths around them. The nearest thing to further digging will be adding a thick layer of garden compost or manure to the surface every back end of the season and lightly forking it in, again from the paths. The hard work will then be carried out by earthworms, bless 'em, who will burrow through your bed, aerating it and carrying the organic material to the lower depths.

Raised beds

These work on the same principle, look very nice and neat, but can be very expensive, especially if you buy the raised bed frames from garden centres. The idea is that you build a frame of timber round your beds, again ideally about four feet wide, using planks not less than six inches deep. If you have four such beds, ten feet long, that is 112 feet of timber. Dig over the bed, adding compost/manure as you go. Then you put in extra topsoil (another cost) so that the bed is raised, i.e. soil level above the surrounding level. Again, you will never stand on the beds after the first digging over and the addition of extra topsoil. I think raised beds are ideal for small gardens, and for larger plots still worth the effort provided you can get the timber free, or money is no object! It was with free timber that the raised beds were created for Newton-le-Willows Gardeners' Association, for example.

Many of us will find it increasingly difficult to bend down or kneel to sow, plant, weed and harvest crops as we get older. Here, Doris Greenhalgh (the author's mother) is preparing a new raised bed that can be tended from a wheelchair or mobility buggy. Of course, in long dry spells, this will need extra watering, though putting plenty of humus in the soil as the bed is filled will help. Incidentally, a raised bed of this size (roughly 6 feet by 3 feet) is large enough to grow a family's salad crops (lettuce, other leaves such as rocket, radish, spring onions and a few baby beetroot) for at least nine months of the year. There is probably also enough room for a few herbs, such as thyme and marjoram.

Two brown winter shoots of couch grass. The smaller (right) has grown from the underground stem (or rhizome) sent out by the larger (left), which is also sending out rihizomes in other directions. In species like couch grass, creeping thistle, horsetail (or mare's tail) and bindweed, if you simply dig over and leave these cut up in the soil, each will produce a new plant. So go through carefully and remove every piece.

SPACE & WHAT YOU CAN GROW

everyone can grow something!

Garden aspect

ALL GREEN PLANTS NEED SOME SUNLIGHT, for, as every school kid knows, it is by photosynthesis that they produce what we eat. Vegetables and most fruits thrive only in full sun, so do not expect to get good crops if the veg plot is shaded by tall trees or is on the north side of the house. Similarly, greenhouses and garden frames should be sited in full sun. Put sheds and compost bins in the shadier corners. Some of the soft fruits (blackberries, raspberries, black- and redcurrants) will give reasonable crops in semi-shade.

Bear this in mind when buying a new house, and if you are not intending to move, investigate ways of increasing the amount of sunlight in certain areas of your garden.

Just about everyone in Lancashire can grow *something* to eat, even if the space available is only a window box.

Parsley is easy to grow in containers.

The smallest

If space is minimal (an apartment balcony, back yard, patio, or just a window box) I would recommend growing salad crops in containers. Taste- and aroma-less lettuce and salad leaves from the supermarket are relatively expensive, but they are a doddle to grow in containers and, provided you have a few different varieties of seeds, you can have a lovely mixture of textures, flavours and aromas through the year. Even though I have lots of garden space, I still grow salad leaf mixtures in 8-inch plant pots, and lettuces in any boxes 6 inches or more deep that I can scrounge, making a sowing every fortnight from February to October. It's also worth growing a few herbs, such as basil, thyme and parsley, in pots, which can sit quite happily on your window sills. You can even have a tomato plant or two in your house, just in a small pot in a sunny room. They look and smell lovely as they grow, flower and fruit.

Modest

You may have a small 'modern' garden that has a lawn and narrow flower beds. Why not plant some vegetables amongst the flowers, or put in a couple of bushes, such as a blackcurrant and redcurrant? Or, to hide an unsightly fence, fix wires along it, and plant some raspberries and a thornless blackberry, training them to the wires.

You might also have a patio, in which case a couple of containers around three feet by two feet can produce a lot of salads (once you get going, enough for a family of four or five from spring to late autumn). Why not have dwarf 'patio' fruit trees in tubs? Or, if you want a newish idea, try a 'veg trug', which is a purpose-built container on legs.

Lettuces and other green salad crops grow very happily in troughs, boxes or enclosed beds – keep a watering can very handy though.

Average

If you have space in your small garden for a plot of around fifteen feet long by three feet wide, then you can grow a nice range of vegetables. But think of flavour and forget vegetables that are inexpensive in Lancashire, such as potatoes, carrots, swedes, onions, winter cabbages and sprouts. Instead, buy these from your nearest farm shop or market and concentrate on the fancier stuff.

Split the plot into three so that you can have crop rotation and try growing things like pak choi, mangetout or sugar snap peas, baby beetroot, French beans, salad crops, spinach, swiss chard, a courgette plant and summer cabbages. Aim for things that grow quickly, so you can resow or plant, and that taste great.

Lucky you!

If you have a large garden (or an allotment) then the choice is yours. If you like asparagus, why not have an asparagus bed? My last one died in 2011 and up to then we had two platefuls twice a week for nine weeks annually over 12 years. I have planted a new one which will give us a crop in 2014.

Even when you have a lot of space, however, you still need to think carefully about using it wisely. Soft fruit is expensive, even at pick-your-own farms, so instead of growing maincrop potatoes and carrots that are almost given away in the region's markets and farm shops, soft fruit is a better use of the land. My five gooseberry and blackcurrant bushes, two redcurrants, single loganberry and blackberry, and row of raspberries, keep us in fruit for pies and puddings throughout the winter and we freeze lots.

If you have an allotment as well as a garden you really are lucky. You may even have space for flowers, especially in your garden.

Always have a bird table and feeders in your GYO plot. The birds will devour many pests.

Other garden spaces

Allotments

There is usually a long waiting list for local authority allotments, so if you want one, go to your council offices and get your name on the list, NOW! There may also be private allotment sites, often associated with working men's clubs and the like. A good website is www.nsalg.org.uk, the National Society of Allotment & Leisure Gardeners. It has lots of advice about how to obtain and maintain an allotment and is a good place to start.

Be aware of the time needed to care for an allotment. Some years ago, when my garden veg plot was still fairly small and the lawn too big, I took over an allotment across the field from home. It had been neglected and I spent the whole of a mild February (I did no other work that month) double-digging it, getting it into beds, constructing compost bins, and so on. Yvonne's father raised his eyebrows and commented, 'You've got all that garden *and* an allotment!' Eventually it was too much. There are only the two of us and we ended up eating at least five sorts of veg every day (ultra-healthy!) and giving stacks away. The ideal, perhaps, is to share an allotment with a good friend, and some local authorities rent 'half allotments' for those who do not need a full one.

Landshare

An alternative is this excellent nationwide scheme, championed by Hugh Fearnley-Whittingstall, among others. People with land that they are not using make it available to those who have none of their own and an agreement is reached between the two parties. You can find out more about it at www.landshare.net.

Allotments are usually monitored regularly, and woe betide anyone who does not keep theirs in good order, they may be expelled.

Growing in containers

Anyone can grow something to eat in a container and, even though I have a fairly big fruit and veg plot, I still use lots of them. Yvonne says that they clutter the place up! At the time of writing I have seven large and three small plastic fish boxes, washed overboard from fishing boats and collected by me from beaches. In 2011 in one of these, I grew a crop of lettuce, followed by a crop of dwarf French beans, followed by six summer cabbages, followed by a crop of winter spinach. I grow all my strawberries in these boxes, and in one, lettuce followed by stump-rooted carrots every spring/summer.

Don't worry too much about the type of container. One of my large plastic water butts sprang a leak, so I cut it in half to create two large tubs. I grew long-rooted carrots in them in the hope that a few would win me a prize at our Gardeners' Association September show; they didn't. Then I planted a gooseberry bush in one and a blackcurrant in the other.

I have accumulated lots of large terracotta pots and plastic tubs over the years. In the former I have two new fig trees and a collection of very old apple varieties in minarette form. In some of the latter I have a couple of dessert gooseberries and a blackcurrant, and in others I grow outdoor tomatoes, climbing French beans, courgettes and very early potatoes. Smaller pots and tubs house all my herbs.

Many gardeners use 'growbags' to raise tomatoes, cucumbers, sweet peppers, aubergines and melons in the greenhouse. I do not. The cheap growbags are useless, for they have only a shallow depth of compost which makes watering tricky; either you give the plants too much or too little. The deeper growbags are far more expensive than the shallow ones and are not too

Herbs are very easy to grow in large containers.

bad, but far better are large pots and tubs. I grow cucumbers and tomatoes in pots 14–16 inches in diameter, melons in 12-inch pots and peppers and aubergines in 10-inch pots.

You will see lots of adverts in the magazines and papers for potato sacks (the seed potatoes are sometimes sold with them). I have done tests comparing potatoes grown in sacks and in similarly sized tubs/pots. The tubs/pots were marginally better.

I have also tried bags for growing strawberries that can be hung on supports against walls, etc. Mine were a failure, for they were battered by south-westerly winds. If you use them (or tomatoes in hanging baskets) they must be put in *very* sheltered corners, and my lowland Lancashire garden does not have such a thing!

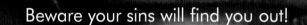

Beware your sins will find you out!

I had been working on some magazine articles in Ireland and, on the Friday evening, was flying back from Belfast city airport to Manchester. A friend was picking me up at Manchester, so I asked Yvonne to go to the allotment when she got home from work and weed the cabbage, sprout and broccoli bed. At 7.15pm the plane crossed the coast at Liverpool but, instead of going directly to the airport, it was 'stacked', flying low over our home and the allotment. I looked down. No sign of Yvonne, but I spotted Old Bill on the neighbouring plot. The plane circled round over Bolton and back towards Lowton. Again I scrutinised both allotment and garden from the air. Definitely no sign of Yvonne. When I arrived home I asked, 'How did the weeding go?'
'Weeding?' she replied.
'You didn't go to the allotment.'
'How do you know?'
'We flew over, twice, and you weren't there!'
After a hard week at work she was just too tired to spend four hours weeding. On Monday I was back in Ireland and she was back to work. It was too much. We gave up the allotment and made our garden plot bigger instead.

Compost for containers

If you have money to burn, buy the very expensive compost sold by DIY stores or garden centres, but I use bought composts only for sowing seeds, potting up young seedlings and for special plants (see below).

There is no doubt that the best commercially available composts are based on peat, but we are trying to get away from peat that comes from endangered peat bogs. I have tried two non-peat composts made from the contents of recycled plant material collected in wheelie-bins. They were terrible! I put two bags of one brand through a half-inch riddle and ended up with less than one bag of reasonable stuff and over a bagful of bits of twig and lumps of wood. I have also found bits of glass and sharp fragments from plastic plant pots in these local authority generated composts. If you use them, always wear a pair of gardening gloves. Currently new composts based on coir are being developed. Coir is waste from the coconut industry.

For growing things like tomatoes, peppers, aubergines, lettuces, stump-rooted carrots, French beans and summer cabbages in containers I use the following mix:

40%	Homemade, well-rotted garden compost
50%	Loam or top soil*
10%	Sharp sand

* *You can buy this, but there are two alternatives: collect soil from mole hills (get the land owner's permission first); or take squares of turf and pile them up in a shady corner. Keep moist (water with very dilute liquid fertiliser or urine) and covered with black polythene. After 12 months they will have rotted down: put through a riddle using the fine sieved loam and put the waste into the compost bin.*

To this I add general fertiliser (if you want an organic alternative to the chemical brands you could try fish, blood and bone) at a

Hidden away behind fruit bushes, mesh enclosures hold great quantities of leaves that will slowly turn into leaf mould, a great soil conditioner and compost.

rate of one handful per large bucket of compost. When the first flower buds appear on tomatoes, peppers, aubergines and beans I water with a tomato fertiliser.

For plants that will remain in the container for a couple of years and more, such as strawberries, fruit bushes (e.g. blackcurrants, gooseberries)and trees (fig, apple minarettes) I use:

80%	John Innes Number 3 (you can buy it by the bag)
20%	homemade garden compost

To this I add a couple of large handfuls of Perlite or grit to every bucket of the mix. This is to improve drainage.

The John Innes contains enough nutrients to last the growing plant up to a month. At this point I give a weak liquid feed every fortnight from April to September using a tomato fertiliser.

For blueberries I use:

95%	Ericaceous compost (which you buy by the bag)
5%	Sharp sand

The only feeding blueberries get are nutrients in my butt water and, in spring and summer, a half-strength helping of liquid ericaceous fertiliser (as recommended for feeding azaleas and rhododendrons). They are bog plants so they do get nutrients from the decomposing compost.

Growing under glass

Here in Lancashire a greenhouse is one of the best things a fruit and veg gardener can buy, for it gives more control over seedling growth, can produce early crops of potatoes, strawberries, French beans, and lettuce, and provides ideal conditions for growing tomatoes, peppers and so on. Everybody buys a greenhouse that is too small – work out the size you think you need and then buy one a size bigger!

Some go one better by purchasing a polytunnel that covers a large proportion of their land, so that most of what they grow is permanently under cover and protected from the ravages of the north-western climate. If I was starting off now I would go for the biggest polytunnel I could fit on my garden plot. But my plot is such an irregular shape, with things that would not fit in a tunnel, that I would have to revamp and I'm too old to do that.

Beware of those little wire-framed polythene 'greenhouses' sold at garden centres. I bought one once and the wind battered it to death! Also the plastic goes brittle and cracks after a spell of frost.

A garden frame is grand for protecting seedlings and for growing short plants such as salad crops and strawberries, and trailing plants like melons. So too are cloches that protect plants growing in rows on the vegetable plot.

BOOSTING GROWTH

fertility is the name of the game!

GIVEN ALL THE HARD WORK THAT WE GARDENERS put into growing crops, it is always good to try to get the very best out of the land we grow on. There is nothing more dispiriting than poor yields or stunted plants after months of effort, but fortunately there are a few things you can do to try to boost growth and productivity.

Crop rotation

If you grow the same crop on the same bed every year you are in for a disaster as disease will beckon. To avoid this we practice three-year crop rotation. This means that one particular crop will be grown in one patch of ground only once in every three years. It is made much easier to practice crop rotation when the vegetable plot is divided up into several non-tread or raised beds, each separated from the others by a path.

The really vulnerable group of crops in the rotation are the brassicas, which include cabbages, cauliflowers, sprouts, broccoli, and the four commonly grown roots – radishes, kohlrabi, swedes and turnips. They can suffer from club root. Get club root into your veg plot and you can forget growing brassicas for at least twenty years.

YEAR ONE	YEAR TWO	YEAR THREE
Lime well just before planting	*Lime only if pH less than 6.5*	*No lime*
		Potatoes
	Onions	Beetroot
Brassicas	Peas and Beans	Carrots
	Sweetcorn and Leeks	Salsify and Scorzonera
	Celeriac and Celery	Parsnips
	Chard and Spinach	
	Courgettes and Marrows	

The list under 'Year Three' is often labelled 'Roots' on crop rotation plans, but that can be confusing because some brassicas (swede, turnip, kohlrabi) are roots and must go with the brassicas. The middle list is often headed 'Others', and that is what it is, everything other than roots and brassicas.

Other published plans often say that manure should not be dug in before growing roots, but manure can be added before planting brassicas and 'others'. Certainly, do not use fresh manure before sowing roots as it may cause the roots to split

or fork. Well-rotted garden compost put on top of the beds (as recommended for no-tread and raised beds) seems to have no such effect.

I draw a map of all my beds every year, so that I know I'm following crop rotation in them all. So in 2013, for example, I sowed my broad beans in a bed that previously had winter cabbages, and new potatoes in a bed that the previous year produced a crop of onions.

Club root: a cautionary tale

My pal John bought a market garden in West Lancashire and, having ploughed it over, he decided that he would give a couple of acres over to spring cabbages. Would I go with him to collect some young plants that were ready for transplanting? Off we went in his van to a farm near Ormskirk, but when I lifted the first batch of plants I saw the malformations in the roots that are the early signs of club root. Now John had never grown anything in his life before, so I told him about club root. But he was not convinced and thought I was exaggerating, and at his insistence we filled the back of the large van with boxes of bare-root young cabbages and headed homewards. But it was a hot day, we were thirsty and the pubs were open. So we stopped off and had a couple. When we got back it was too late to plant the poor things so we planted them the following morning. Over half the plants died within the week from dehydration. The rest succumbed to club root.

Making your own garden compost

Everyone who has a garden ought to do this, for it is the ultimate in recycling, and can save you a fortune. Most local councils these days will provide you with a free composting bin designed to keep under your sink, so you can easily collect your organic waste daily. I use biodegradeable compost liners in these, so the whole lot can just be tipped onto your compost heap.

Anything that has lived can be composted, but avoid all meats as they attract verminous flies, though I do put prawn and shrimp husks and crab shells into the compost heap as they seem to act as an accelerant. So, in go all fine prunings, potato tops, lawn mowings, bean and pea plants after they have been harvested, annuals from the flower garden, peelings from the kitchen, apple cores, lemon slices from the previous evening's G&T – any plant material that would otherwise be thrown away. Of course, this includes weeds, and some weeds will have seeds, while others (e.g. couch grass rhizomes) are tough old plants which may survive composting. To prevent this, put weeds into a bucket of water as you pull them up and leave them to rot down for a few days. Then pour weeds and water into the compost bin. That fetid lot will help accelerate the composting process nicely. Note too that paper and cardboard (made from plant cellulose) should be added to the compost bin not in a deep layer, but mixed in with the soft plant material. Try getting a mix of 60% soft, green plants and 40% paper/cardboard. Shredded bank documents go straight in. Other paper and cardboard should be torn into small pieces and soaked in water. A little soil also helps, so scatter a little into the bin every

Compost bins are best tucked away in a corner of the plot, behind fruit bushes and trees that mask them through the summer.

six inches unless there are plant remains with soil attached to the roots. The better the mix the better the compost.

There are several ways of getting your collection turned into garden compost.

The traditional way is to construct a cuboid bin using old bits of wood. In a big bin (say 4 × 4 × 4 feet plus) the centre can get very hot which means that seeds etc. are killed. After a few weeks you are meant to turn this composting material so that the outside becomes the inside and also gets the heat treatment.

For two years I made some excellent compost using a bin made from straw bales. The sides were three bales long, the ends two bales and the height was two bales, so the bin used twenty bales in all. In the middle went all the composing material. When I came to use this the following late winter and spring, even the bales were nearly all composted. Unless you have some good farming friends I think you'll find that these days straw bales are too expensive.

The modern way is to use Dalek-type plastic composting bins and I now have five of them, so that always at least one contains compost ready for use. The little sliding door at the bottom is a waste of time. When the compost is ready to use, I just pull the bin off the pile or fork it out from the top.

You might use something at the start to accelerate the composing process. You can buy accelerators if you are wealthy, but equally good are chicken droppings, weak liquid fertiliser and, dare I say it, dilute human urine.

If the heap is getting on the dry side, water it. But you do not want a foul-smelling soggy mass. It should be moist and not sopping wet.

Fertilisers

Plants need nutrients in the soil if they are going to produce of their best and, while the soil itself and any manure/garden compost we use will add some, we must add extra nutrients in the form of fertiliser. There are two broad categories, depending on your attitude to growing things: organic ('green') and inorganic.

Organic fertilisers

These are made from things that have lived or have been produced by living things. Manures are an example, for they usually have plenty of nitrogen (N) and some phosporus (P) and potassium (K). Chicken manure is especially strong in nitrogen and can burn the roots of plants when fresh. I use this, when I can get it, mixed in the compost bins. (When I was in my teens I helped out on a chicken farm near Woodplumpton, where the farmer built a new muck-heap next to two old ash trees. They were dead a year later.)

Fish, blood and bone and bone meal can be purchased at garden centres etc. The first is a better fertiliser for the GYO gardener as it contains a wider range of nutrients. Seaweed (either fresh or dried and processed) is also well worth using if you want to be an organic grower. You may not remove fresh seaweed from coastal areas without permission from the landowner or council, but if you do have access to a plentiful supply it can be dug into your soil in the same way as farmyard manure. It will go slimy if left on the surface, however, so it is best to dig it into the soil when it is still wet. Alternatively, put it in the compost heap.

Mushroom compost may be useful in gardens with acid soil.

A good growing medium for container-grown vegetables is made by mixing leaf mould with garden compost.

Making an 'organic' liquid feed

FEED 1: Put lots of comfrey or nettle shoots into an old dustbin and fill up with water. Leave for a couple of weeks, and then water with the resulting juice diluted to the colour of lager.

FEED 2: Get a hessian sack full of sheep droppings (you can gather these easily from heavily-grazed moorland or saltmarshes) and suspend this in an old dustbin full of water.

Leave for a couple of weeks before using (1 cupful in a gallon of water). Great for brassicas. Not great for neighbours.

The drawback to these homemade organic fertilisers is that you can't be sure that everything the plant needs is there, and usually the concentrations of things like the essential N, P and K are low. But try the comfrey juice; it works well with leafy vegetables.

Nettles make great compost.

Inorganic fertilisers

These are produced from pure chemicals and they have the great advantage over organic ones in that you know precisely what nutrients you are giving to your crops. Growmore is the best known general fertiliser with a balance of N, P and K plus other nutrients. If growing potatoes, use the special potato fertiliser (N14, P14, K21) or onions, the onion fertiliser (N11, P22, K22) for better results, and for brassicas N27, P6 K6. Provided you follow the manufacturers' instructions, your plants will benefit from their use. Specialist fertilisers (e.g. tomato fertiliser, which has the nutrients essential for all fruit-producing crops) are usually inorganic. BUT plant roots take up the nutrients that the plant wants from the soil selectively, so that it will take only what it needs. This means that, no matter what you use, provided that you follow the instructions given on the packet, the stuff that you eat will depend on the plant. Of course, the problem with pure chemicals is that they can damage the soil when too much is put on; that, of course, doesn't really matter if used for plants growing in containers, which is why I am happy to use commercial tomato liquid feed.

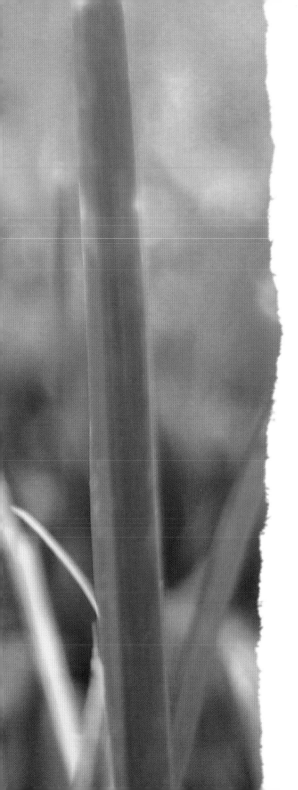

WEEDS, PESTS & PROBLEMS

weeding is such fun!

VEGETABLE PLOT SOIL IS PERFECT for growing weeds as well as vegetables, and because weeds compete with our crops for water, nutrients and light, we must remove them as they grow – or outwit them! – in the following ways.

Growing plants through black polythene

After preparing the soil, cover with black polythene, cut holes in the polythene and plant through those holes. This works well for potatoes, brassicas and strawberries, but not for things like peas or beetroot. Part of my plot was overrun with horsetail (also known as mare's tail) and by growing this way I knocked out much of this pernicious weed by keeping the black polythene in place for 12 months.

Using the chemical glyphosate

This is completely broken down the moment it touches the soil so it is harmless other than to green plant material it touches. If it is drifted by the wind onto your crop, however, your crop will suffer,

43

so use the large plastic drink bottle method. Cut the bottom off the bottle and place the remainder, neck up, over the weed until it touches the soil, enclosing the weed completely. Then spray the glyphosate onto the weed via the bottle neck. You can also 'paint' the glyphosate on with a small paintbrush if the weed is growing too close to your plant to use the bottle method safely.

Hand weed

This may seem laborious but it is easy when you have narrow beds. As I am aging, I try to use one of the kneeling stools specially designed for this task, though as you can see opposite, I don't always follow my own advice! Put the weeds, as you pull them up, into a bucket of water and, before putting them on the compost heap, leave for two or three days for them to die and begin to rot. This will kill their seeds which may otherwise survive composting.

Hoe hoe hoe!

Use a long-handled hoe where there are spaces between the plants, but beware of damaging shallow roots and the necks of things like parsnips and salsify.

Boxing clever

There is a way you can avoid weeding AND improve the soil in one fell swoop, provided that the crop is going to be there for several months (e.g. kale, sprouts, Savoy cabbages, celeriac) or years (fruit trees and bushes). I have also done this with my rose beds.

First of all, give the bed a good weeding, then cover it with well-soaked cardboard, leaving a little gap around each plant. (This, of course, is why I like to carry my shopping home from farm shops and supermarkets in cardboard boxes, and buy most of the wine we drink by mail order!) Cover the cardboard with a mulch – very well-rotted muck, homemade compost, leaf mould, spent mushroom compost, that sort of thing. This will prevent those dreadful ephemeral and annual weeds from growing from the seeds on the soil. Eventually the cardboard will decay and go with the compost underground, care of the lovely earthworms, to benefit the roots of later crops. Of course, you should be composting every bit of plant waste your home and garden/allotment generate, mixing plant with brown material, such as cardboard.

RECIPE

Nettle pesto

25g WHITE BREADCRUMBS § 125g YOUNG NETTLES § 1 GARLIC CLOVE, CRUSHED § approx 175ml OLIVE OIL § 25g PARMESAN, GRATED § 15g PINENUTS, TOASTED & FINELY CRUSHED § SEA SALT, BLACK PEPPER

Heat oven to 180°c/Gas Mark 4. Spread breadcrumbs on a baking tray and bake for around 10 minutes, stirring them 2 or 3 times during this time. When golden brown, remove from the oven and put to one side to cool.

Nip off the thinnest (and therefore tenderest) stalks and leaves (I wear washing up gloves to avoid being stung!) and rinse with cold water. Fill a bowl with very cold water and place near your hob. Bring a large, half-full pan of water to the boil and stuff the nettles in with a spoon etc. until they are all totally underwater. Cook for 1 minute, no more, then drain through a sieve and immediately plunge the nettles into the bowl of cold water. Once they are cold, remove and squeeze them until they are as dry as possible – you don't need gloves because cooking removes the stings.

If you have one, put the nettles into a food processor and add the breadcrumbs, parmesan, pinenuts and garlic. With the machine on low speed, slowly drizzle in olive oil until you have a fairly sloppy mixture. (You can use a pestle and mortar to combine the nettles, pinenuts, breadcrumbs, parmesan and garlic, adding the oil bit by bit and mixing in between if you don't have a food processor.)

Add salt and pepper to taste. Serve with crusty bread, on bruschetta or use as a simple sauce for pasta.

Slugs & Snails

These slimy little pests will quite merrily eat your crops if you let them. Do not scatter metaldehyde slug pellets everywhere, though, for any other animal eating those poisoned slugs (song thrushes, hedgehogs, frogs) may themselves suffer or die. There are several other brands of slug killers on the market, containing iron salts, that do not have this effect. You could also try the half orange/lemon/grapefruit trick (squeeze out the juice first). Put them, sliced side down, amongst the crops and kill the slugs that are attracted to them. Or the stale beer trap: pour beer in shallow jars set out amongst the plants. The slugs go for a drink, get tiddly and fall in and drown. You will need to check your slug traps regularly, on a daily basis if possible. Note too that untidy gardens, with lots of dead and dying bits of plants lying around, generate more slugs than a tidy, clean garden.

Other pests

Solving the problem of certain specific pests is given elsewhere, such as carrot root fly, blackfly on broad beans and codlin moth on apples. Some general points are given here, however.

First, a tidy garden will have fewer problems than an untidy one.

Second, it is not always necessary to use chemical sprays. Examine brassicas every day or two and crush the tiny yellow eggs and caterpillars of white butterflies, the brown caterpillars of cabbage moth, and greenfly on things like the tips of rose shoots. Or enclose your growing crops in netting through which these pests cannot get. I have made simple frames from bits of wood that enclose a section of my narrow no-tread beds and covered these with netting. These keep not only nasty insects away, but also neighbours' cats that might otherwise use the beds as latrines, and wood pigeons that can devour a few cabbage plants in an hour.

Also make sure that you have nest boxes up for blue tits and for those solitary bees that prey on insect pests. In the greenhouse, use sticky fly paper to capture flying pests, such as whitefly. I have never used the commercially available parasites of major insect pests, as I have never found the need to go to that expense.

Note that, if a plant is growing healthily, a bit of pest damage will not harm it. Of course, if you want to go in for competitions at the local show, your vegetables must look perfect. But most of us mainly go for flavour, and happily ignore blemishes – unlike our supermarkets, which mostly sell beautiful but relatively tasteless stuff.

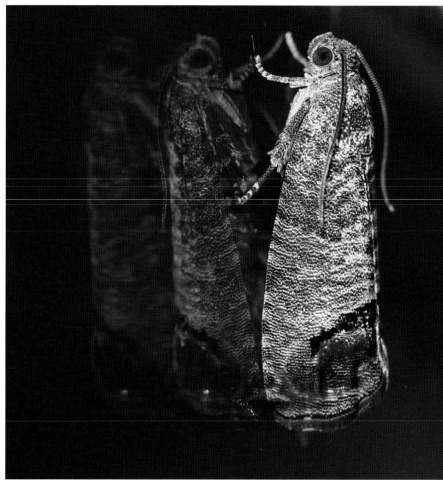

Cabbage white butterflies (left) and cabbage moth (above) are the curse of brassica-growing, for their caterpillars can shred a cabbage or sprout plant in no time at all. You could use sprays. Far better, cover the crops with insect-proof netting, making sure there are no gaps. Or crush the eggs and tiny caterpillars.

Another good way to combat destructive insects is to encourage those that are on our side! One of the best-known is our friend the ladybird. These beautiful little creatures consume large numbers of greenfly and other aphids, both when adult and as larvae.

PART
TWO

VEGETABLE SOWING, PLANTING & HARVESTING

the wild & savage North West

MOST GARDENING BOOKS AND MAGAZINE ARTICLES are written by folk who live in the soft, dry and warmer climate of southern England and the Midlands, so that we who live here in this less forgiving (but wonderful) part of our country must be careful when following their advice. It is, for instance, said that it is OK sowing broad beans in late autumn, but over much of our region many of the seeds may rot in the cold, wet soil. An early spring-sown crop will do much better. The books also tell us that cucumbers can be grown outside easily, but for us this is true only in warm summers and close to the coast.

What follows is a veg-by-veg guide to the sowing and harvesting times that are best for the North West, which should help to keep your crops safe from the vagaries of our climate – although given some of the freak conditions of the last few years there can be no guarantees!

I then deal with the vegetables that you should be able to succeed with, giving you as many useful tips as I can on sowing, cropping and general care.

BEANS, BROAD   Sow late February–March. Harvest late June–August.

BEANS, FRENCH   Sow late May–early July. Harvest August–October. (An earlier crop can be had by sowing in the warmth of a heated greenhouse or kitchen window sill in April and growing on in a container in the cold greenhouse.)

BEANS, RUNNER   Sow in a frost-free greenhouse in late April–May in pots. Plant out late May–June. Harvest July to first frosts.

BEETROOT   Sow the end of April–early July. Harvest August–November.

BROCCOLI, PURPLE-SPROUTING   Sow early varieties April–May, late varieties late May–June (see Note at end). Harvest September– April depending on variety. If you have space, grow 4–5 plants of both early and late varieties to give a long cropping season.

CALABRESE BROCCOLI   Sow late April–early May in a seed-bed or in modules and plant out in June. Harvest August–October.

BRUSSELS SPROUT   Different varieties mature at different times, so if you want to eat GYO sprouts throughout the September–March season you must grow more than one variety. Sow some seeds of an early variety under glass in the first half of March, the others in late March– April. Plant out May–June. Harvest end September–early March.

CABBAGE, SUMMER   Sow a very few seeds late February (under cover), late March and late April/early May; most families will find that producing four seedlings to plant out for each of the three sowing times will be enough for their needs, unless they are cabbageoholics – and there are only so many things you can do with a cabbage! Plant out end April, end May and second half of June. Harvest late June or July–end September or early October. In 2012 I sowed a pinch of seeds in late January and planted four of the

seedlings in a box in the greenhouse; they were ready to eat in late April and early May.

CABBAGE, WINTER/SAVOY/RED   Sow late April–May. Plant out July. Harvest Red in September–October, Winter; Savoy in October–February.

CABBAGE, SPRING   Sow the end of July or early August. Plant out first half October. Harvest March–early May.

CARROTS   Sow stump-rooted varieties in February in containers in cold greenhouse. Harvest from May onwards. Sow other carrots outside March–early July. Harvest July–November. Keep covered with fleece to avoid carrot fly attack!

CAULIFLOWER   Sow February under glass, April–early May outside. Plant out early sowing varieties the beginning of April, others June–July. Harvest mid June–early September. The late sowing and planting times also apply to autumn- and winter- maturing varieties.

CUCUMBER   If you can provide a temperature of 21°C+/70°F+ then sow in early March; otherwise buy a plant or two from a garden centre. Plant in a cold greenhouse the second half of May. Harvest mid June onwards.

FLORENCE (OR BULB) FENNEL   Sow April–June. Harvest June–September.

KALE   Try it! It's a useful winter veg. Sow late April–early May. Plant out July. Harvest end November through winter.

KOHLRABI (alias 'sputniks'!)   Sow a few seeds at regular intervals mid April–July (few families will want to eat a rowful at one sitting). Harvest July–November.

LEEK   If you want to grow leeks for the full season of September–April, you must grow three varieties, one early, one mid season and one late. But the sowing and planting out times are similar. Sow mid March–mid April. Plant out June–early July. Harvest earlies September–November, mid season varieties the end of November–January, late season late January onwards.

LETTUCE   For an early crop (April–May) sow in February on a frost-free window sill and plant and grow on in the cold greenhouse from mid March. Otherwise, for a summer/autumn crop sow late March–early July, and harvest June–early October. To have lettuces ready in time for Christmas, sow a suitable variety early August.

MARROW, COURGETTE, PUMPKIN AND SQUASH   Sow in warmth (a window sill is ideal) at the end of April and plant out in early June, or sow where they will grow outside at the end of May (or buy plants from a garden centre). Harvest courgettes from July, mature fruits up to the end of October.

ONION FROM SETS   Plant end March–April, for harvest late July–August. Plant over-wintering varieties September–early October for harvest late May–June.

ONIONS FROM SEED   Sow in frost-free indoors January–February. Prick-out into plastic modules or 2-inch pots when the seedlings resemble a shepherd's crook and then into 3-inch pots when the roots are filling the 2-inch one. Plant out late April. Harvest July–August.

PARSNIP   Sow in mid March–mid April in deep holes filled with compost. Harvest October–February.

PEA, GARDEN   Sow under glass (in a greenhouse or under cloches) end February; harvest late May and June. Sow outside end March–early April; harvest late June–July. Sow early May; harvest August–early September.

PEA, MANGETOUT AND SUGAR SNAP   Sow April–May; harvest late July–early August.

POTATO PLANT   'Seed' in frost-free place, in 10-inch pots, in February; harvest April–May. Plant outdoors April; harvest first earlies late June on, second earlies and maincrop from early August on.

RADISH   Sow under cover February–early March; harvest April. Sow outdoors late March–July; harvest May–September.

SALSIFY AND SCORZONERA   Sow second half April; harvest October–February. Well worth growing as you hardly ever see these for sale, yet they taste great.

SPINACH   Sow late March–May and mid August–September (it runs to seed quickly from a summer sowing); harvest possible through much of the year (cover with cloches in winter).

SWEDE   Sow last week May or first week June; harvest October–February.

SWEETCORN   Sow in warmth under glass at the end of April, in peat pots or the cardboard insides of loo rolls. Plant out early June. Harvest August–early September.

TOMATO   A good outdoor crop can never be guaranteed in Lancashire. For a cold greenhouse crop, sow early March–early April in frost-free place (e.g. a window sill), transplant early May, harvest July onwards.

TURNIP   Sow April–June, harvest June–September.

Asparagus

Well worth it if you like asparagus and have plenty of room, for to grow twenty plants in two rows you will need a bed a good four or five feet wide and twenty feet long. Such a bed should produce a good crop over at least ten years. Steamed, with butter, salt and black pepper, asparagus is a gourmet's delight. Once you have tasted asparagus cut and immediately cooked and enjoyed, you will never buy that waste of air-miles, tasteless, imported stuff again!

PLANTING   Prepare the bed in winter, by double-digging and incorporating as much garden compost/rotted manure as you can and removing stones and weeds. In my gley clay soil, I also dug in four bags of sharp sand on a plot of this size, to increase drainage. Buy crowns – sowing seeds wastes years! Plant these as soon as you get them home, with the tip of the crown 3 inches below the surface, 12–18 inches apart and spacing the rows 24 inches apart. Apply a general fertiliser when planting. Then as the fern grows, add more soil so that the bed is raised.

CROPPING   In the first year after planting take no crop, but give a weak liquid feed monthly and keep well watered in dry weather. In year two take a very small crop: all the spears that grow up to the second week of May. Cut 2–3 inches beneath the soil surface (you can buy a special knife for this purpose). Thereafter, take ALL spears up to eight or nine weeks after they first appear; in my

Lancashire garden, this has varied from 5 April (2011) to 28 April (1999).

AFTER CROPPING   Give a liquid feed to encourage fern growth, so that next year's crop will have lots of stores laid down underground. In windy sites, give the fern plenty of support (canes, twine, netting).

Go for Mondeo, or Pacific 2000, or (for big yields) Ariane.

Beans

Four types of bean grow well in northern gardens: broad beans, dwarf French beans, climbing French beans and runner beans. All can be frozen, so that a large crop can be enjoyed long into the winter; though, like many, I find frozen runner beans watery and relatively tasteless and so freeze French types instead. Beans and peas usually prefer soil that is neutral or slightly alkaline (pH 6.5–7), so a dusting of ground limestone or lime may be appropriate. Scatter a general fertiliser before sowing.

Broad

SOWING   Some books suggest sowing in late autumn, but it is not worth doing so in Lancashire and neighbouring counties. A crop sown in March will catch up with any sown earlier and the losses will be fewer. It is also worth using controlled germination. Put the seeds into a polythene bag containing moist seed compost. Check every day and, as soon as the radicles (young roots) begin to emerge from the seed, with the longest no more than ¼ inch long, sow them. Sow the seeds 8 inches apart, 3 inches deep in a double row 8 inches apart. If you want to sow another double row, that should be 24 inches from the first double row. Some seeds may not have an emerging radicle; sow them close together at the end of the rows so that, should some seeds in the rows not produce plants, gaps can be filled in by transplanting the ones at the end.

VARIETIES   Green Windsor is a lovely tasting bean; also Imperial Green Longpod, Masterpiece Green Longpod and Express. In windswept gardens grow The Sutton, a short-growing but good-cropping variety.

CARE: 1. The plants will need support. Garden string, stretched at three heights between canes put in around each double row, is ideal.
2. In a drought, water well when the first flowers appear.
3. The tips of broad bean plants often become infested with blackfly towards the end of flowering time. Pinch out the tips (and any blackflies that are there) and compost them.

HARVEST   In a crop sown March–April, harvesting is usually late June–August. I prefer smaller softer beans, so pick mine earlier than most. Others like large harder beans. They freeze well – blanch first for 1–2 minutes.

POST HARVEST   Cut the haulms at ground level and compost them. The roots have nitrogen-rich nodules which contribute to the next crop so leave them in the ground. Plant chard, spinach, lettuce, salad leaves or a late lot of leeks after harvesting the beans.

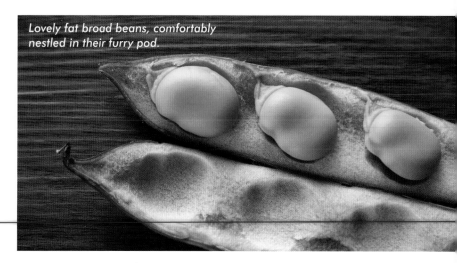

Lovely fat broad beans, comfortably nestled in their furry pod.

French

SOWING   French bean seeds will rot in cold and/or waterlogged ground, so here in the North West wait until the second or third week of May to sow them outside, with the last sowing in late June or (coastal areas) early July. My first crop of lettuces are grown in a fish box in the cold greenhouse and they are usually all eaten by the middle of April, so I follow them immediately with dwarf French bean plants, sown in plant pots on the kitchen window sill the third week of March. This gives a crop of lovely beans in June. Outside, sow the seeds, 1 inch deep, 4 inches apart, in rows 18 inches apart. Dwarf varieties need some support (2 foot high bits of twiggy branch or string and canes) otherwise they tend to flop on the ground. Climbing varieties need a frame or wigwam.

VARIETIES   The Prince and Masterpiece are good old varieties of dwarf French bean; Montano and Parker. Newer ones, Cobra and Hunter are climbing French beans.

CARE: 1. Water well, especially during flowering.
2. Feeding with tomato fertiliser once a week when flowering is under way will prolong the cropping time (to as late as the first frosts).

HARVEST   When not too big! They freeze well; pod, and blanch for one minute before putting in freezer bags.

Runner

SOWING   Runners will be killed by any frost, so in Pennine valleys always sow under cover in mid May and plant out in mid June. Even in the lowlands sowing in a greenhouse or on the kitchen window sill is safest and tends to produce healthy vigorous plants that grow quickly when planted out. Sow in deep tubes (the cardboard tube insides of toilet rolls are perfect, cost nothing, and will rot down when the young plants are put out), 2 inches deep. Runner beans need lots of water, so add a lot of organic material into the runner bean bed in late winter.

PLANTING OUT   9 inches apart at the foot of supporting canes (see CARE).

VARIETIES   Enorma and Red Knight are both excellent; White Lady has white flowers and great flavours.

CARE: 1. They need support up to 8 feet high. This can be a wigwam or frame made from 8 foot canes or (better) bean poles made from hazel or ash. Make sure that such supports are well anchored in place, for strong winds will flatten weak supports, especially when laden with fully grown runner beans.

2. Water well and keep weed-free.
3. Nip out plant tips when they reach the top of the supports.
4. In dry weather spraying the flowers with a mist of water will enhance setting of the bean pods.

HARVEST   Pick the beans when still young and tender; they are then at their best for flavour. I give excess away and in 2010 six plants fed us and five neighbours twice a week for six weeks! Freeze French beans but not runners.

Runner beans in flower – to encourage a good 'set', spray daily.

Beetroot

SOWING   In good soil, raking a general fertiliser in just before sowing. Although in milder parts of the country sowings can be made in March (using the variety Boltardy), here in Lancashire, sowings from mid April to early July are most successful. I once sowed one row in mid March under a cloche, and another, in mid April, and the latter almost caught up the earlier sowing. Beetroot seeds have a germination inhibitor in the seed-case which is washed out by water, so soak the seeds for a few hours before sowing. In droughts water well until the first leaves have emerged from the ground after germination. Or use the wet kitchen roll technique: take a couple of pieces of paper kitchen roll and put them on a plate; sandwich the beetroot seeds in between; wet the paper thoroughly; peek at the seeds daily and when the tiny white roots are just beginning to emerge, sow carefully. Then water in. Sow 2 seeds every 2 inches in drills (rows) ½–¾ inch deep, with drills 12 inches apart; thin to one plant per station after germination.

VARIETIES   Try Boltardy and one of the Detroit strains (Little Ball for 'baby beetroot' and New Globe for larger 'show' beetroot). Newer varieties that have great flavour include Cardeal F1 and Pablo F1.

CARE: 1. Keep weeded and water in dry spells.
2. Watering with a salt solution (a level dessert spoon of salt per gallon of water) as the beets are swelling is said to improve colour and flavour, but experiments by the RHS showed that this was a fallacy.

The books usually recommend sowing in seedbeds, but I find it more convenient to sow a few seeds of each variety, ½ inch deep, in good seed compost in seed trays or shallow 3-inch pots. When these have germinated and the two rounded seed leaves are well developed, I prick these out individually into 3-inch pots using the same good quality seed compost. When the roots have filled these small pots (about a fortnight) I plant on similarly into 5-inch pots. This may seem fiddly, but most families need relatively few of each (see below), so the effort is not too great, and this method does grow strong and healthy plants.

CARE: 1. Plant out into their final positions when the roots are filling the pot.
2. The brassica bed should have been prepared with lots of compost in autumn/early winter, limed (with ground limestone) in late winter, and had a general fertiliser raked in just before planting.
3. Dig a hole for each plant and dust the hole with lime to discourage club root; then plant a little deeper than when in the pot and firm well.
4. Slip a collar (commercially available) around the stem to prevent cabbage root fly attack. Water well.
5. For tall plants – Brussels sprouts, broccoli – stake and tie in as the plants grow to prevent the wind damaging the roots/stem.
6. Cover with fine netting to prevent cabbage white butterflies laying their eggs on your plants, or check carefully every couple of days and crush any yellow butterfly eggs and caterpillars.

HARVEST   Take every other beetroot when tiny as baby beets (delicious as a boiled vegetable) and allow the others to grow to the size of a golf ball before harvesting them.

Leave the last sowing in the ground and take them through the autumn when needed; early or mid November, dig up the rest and store in dry sand in a frost-free place.

Brassicas

Because their cultivation and problems are similar, we will deal with cabbages, cauliflower, sprouts, broccoli and kale together. We will then deal with brassica 'roots' – kohlrabi, swede, turnip and radish – for they too share the same problems.

In wet years (as 2012) nitrogen in the soil is quickly washed away and without nitrogen these leafy vegetables will not grow. So, give growing winter and spring cabbages, sprouts, broccoli and kale a boost of nitrogenous fertiliser (sulphate of ammonia if you are not growing organically, or fish, blood and bone if you are) in August and/or September if the rain continues to fall.

Broccoli, sprouting

SOWING   Sow April or early May and plant out June – early July, 24 inches apart in rows 24 inches apart. Firm the soil well and stake and tie in as they grow. If you sow earlier, Purple Sprouting varieties may produce their sprouts earlier, in autumn.

VARIETIES   Early Purple Sprouting and Late Purple Sprouting are the main varieties, providing fresh veg in February–April when other vegetables are in poor supply. They are a highlight of the year, on a par with asparagus, served with butter, salt and pepper. Calabrese (or green sprouting broccoli) produces heads in late summer–autumn; Iron man, Express Corona, Green Comet and Monterey are good F1 varieties.

Purple broccoli plants with fast-growing turnips. Late purple broccoli is harvested when other veg are in short supply, it tastes lovely, freshly cut and served with butter, and it is very expensive in the shops. Note the butterfly-proof netting.

Brussels sprouts

SOWING   Sow mid April and plant out the beginning of June, 30 inches apart in rows 30 inches apart. Firm the soil very well; loosely planted sprout plants often do not produce good tight sprouts. Stake the plants well and tie in as they grow.

VARIETIES   Always grow F1 hybrid sprouts (it will say F1 on the packet alongside the variety name). If you have space for only three or four plants, you want one that will be perfect for Christmas: Widgeon is first choice, with Cascade second. If you want an earlier variety (September on), choose Peer Gynt or Maximus. And for a very late variety try Fortress or Montgomery.

Spring Cabbage

SOWING   Sow August to plant out September–early October, 6 inches apart in rows 12 inches apart (so for a 10 foot row you

need 20 plants). In early spring take every other plant and use as 'spring greens', then let the others develop hearts.

VARIETY   Pixie and Pyramid are excellent, Wheeler's Imperial is an old but also top quality variety.

Winter/savoy Cabbage

SOWING   April–May to plant out in mid June–July, 18 inches apart in rows 24 inches apart. Eat from September onwards.

VARIETY   Tundra is excellent (and butterflies are not too keen on it), Ormskirk is a real Lancashire variety.

Unless you want to grow very large cabbages for the show, plant them closer than the seed packet says. Few families can devour a show-winning mammoth at one sitting.

By growing brassicas under very fine 'enviromesh' you prevent cabbage white butterflies laying their eggs.

Summer Cabbage

SOWING   Sow from late February (on a sunny window sill) to the middle of May. I make three sowings, each generating four plants in pots, the first sowing late February, the second early April, the third mid May. The growing plants are planted out the end of April, end of May and end of June respectively, 12 inches apart in rows 12 inches apart (often in my fish boxes or other large containers). They are eaten May–September. As an experiment in 2012 I sowed a pinch of seed at the end of January, potted them on and finally planted four in a box 30 inches by 15 inches by 10 inches deep in the greenhouse; we ate the first at the end of April.

VARIETY   Greyhound and Hispi are well-proven varieties.

Cauliflower

I used to find growing caulies very difficult. This was probably because of my clay soils – I know some farmers on the peaty mosslands and on the flat silt fields backing the Ribble estuary who find growing caulies a doddle! The clue, they told me, was to give the plants lots of water. 2011 and 2012 confirmed this, for in those wet summers I tried that lovely variety Romanesco Veronica F1, and every egg a bird! So in future, if we go more than a week without rain, my caulies will get lots of water.

SOWING   April-June (I sow a few seeds every month, each time raising six plants in pots before planting out), 24 inches apart. When the curds (the white heads) begin to develop,

For perfect cauliflowers, water regularly and feed well.

bend down some of the bigger leaves to protect them. Harvest July onwards. If you wish, with the variety All the Year Round, you could sow as early as January (in warmth) to get a June crop.

VARIETIES   All the Year Round is a good old variety of white cauliflower, but for flavour nothing beats Romanesco Veronica F1.

A big, top quality show cabbage. But can you imagine a family of four or five tackling this with roast beef, roast spuds and Yorkshire Pudding for Sunday lunch? And what would you cook it in?

Florence Fennel

In recent years, bulb fennel has appeared more often on market stalls and in supermarkets. But, it wasn't until Jean said, "Can we grow some fennel?", on the association's experimental plot in 2013 that I had grown it.

SOWING April–June, half an inch deep in a row.

VARIETY Tauro F1 ... make sure you use F1 seeds.

CARE Keep well watered. Thin out to 8 inches apart and harvest when the bulbs are almost touching.

HARVEST Late June–July from an April sowing, August from a May spowing, September from a June sowing. For the average family, a short row resulting in about 6 plants per sowing is ideal. If left the plants can run to seed easily.

Kale

SOWING Sow in late April or early May and plant out in July, 18 inches apart in rows 18 inches apart.

VARIETIES Kale is really a winter vegetable and is now becoming acceptable to people who until recently thought it only fit for cattle. Try Nero di Toscana, Redbor and Winterbor. Start harvesting in autumn, picking the leaves you need. New leaves will form that can be picked later in the winter. When the hard winter of 2010–11 killed all but one of my broccoli plants and all but two of my winter cabbages, my kale plants thrived.

Brassica roots

Kohlrabi

Though not common in supermarkets, kohlrabi is often sold in our indoor and outdoor markets. It is quite different in taste to swede and turnip and well worth growing in a large garden/allotment, and is easier to grow than turnips if your soil dries out quickly. Kohlrabi does look a bit like a turnip, but to me they look most like sputniks – those little spherical objects launched into space by the Russions in the 1950s! Taste-wise, I think they are very similar to the inside of a broccoli stem, and they can be eaten raw, grated into salads, or sauted, steamed, roasted or baked in a gratin with thyme and spinach. Yum.

SOWING   Make two sowings, one in mid April and one in mid June to harvest in late June–early September. Sow thinly in drills ½ inch deep, with rows 12 inches apart. Keep well watered

Kholrabi – or vegetable sputnik, as I like to call it! This is a perfect 'show' specimen. For the table, harvest at half this size.

and harvest when quite small – a bit larger than a golf ball, and under no circumstances bigger than a tennis ball, otherwise they are likely to be quite woody.

VARIETIES   Green/White Vienna is an old one, but new F1 hybrids such as Olivia and Rowel have slightly better flavour.

Radish

The perfect plant for children to grow, for sowing to harvesting is so quick … and they can be grown in large pots or shallow tubs.

SOW   Radishes could almost be sown year round, provided you can keep them warm in winter, but they are usually sown in very short rows or tiny patches of ground late March to July for harvesting around 25 days later (don't leave them too long). There are special winter varieties, but I have never found anyone who grows them!

VARIETIES   French Breakfast and Scarlet Globe are equal first!

Swede

A fine winter vegetable but not too expensive in the shops; so grow only if you have plenty of land.

SOW   In the second half of May, in drills ½ inch deep, with rows 15 inches apart, for a harvest October onwards; thin out to 9 inches apart as the young plants grow. Water well.

VARIETY   Marian is the best!

The humble swede – delicious mashed with butter, black pepper and nutmeg and served with haggis and tatties!

Turnip

Remember that turnips are brassicas. This is important because they grow so quickly that they are often used as a catch crop: one to grow when some space appears following the harvest of another. But turnips must not be grown on ground that has had any brassica growing on it in the previous two years (ditto kohlrabi, radish and swede, see page 33–4), and you must not grow any other brassica in the same soil for two years after growing turnips.

SOW   Sowings from the second half of March to August will give crops two to three months later. Sow in drills ½ inch deep, with rows 12 inches apart and thin sowings in March–April so that plants are 9–12 inches apart. Keep well watered. Harvest early sowings at or slightly bigger than golf ball size, later at tennis ball size.

VARIETIES   Snowball is best for March–April sowings, Golden Ball or Purple Top Milan for later sowings.

Leeks

If you have a reasonable-sized garden or allotment, leeks are well worth growing, for they taste better when cooked immediately after harvesting. If you have a small garden, don't grow leeks for they are inexpensive in Lancashire farm shops, although somewhat pricier in supermarkets.

SOWING   March or early April. I sow them ½ inch deep in seed trays; others sow them in a seed bed in the garden.

VARIETY   Musselburgh is an old and popular variety, but some of the newer F1 varieties, such as Megaton (matures autumn) followed by Belton (over winter), followed by Kenton (to spring) are far better.

CARE   If sown in a seed bed, thin the seedlings to 2 inches apart. If sown in a seed tray, when they at the hooked stage, just after gemination, transplant the seedlings carefully into seed trays, 3 inches apart. I keep these in the greenhouse until the end of April or early May, when I move them outside still in their trays 'to harden off' (get used to the open air) and give them a weak liquid feed. By mid May or when the leek plants are about as thick as a pencil, I plant them in the ground.

The easiest way of planting out leeks is to have a thick 'dibber' (mine is a broken spade handle) which will make a 6 inch deep round hole in the well-cultivated ground. Make a hole, drop in a leek seedling and pour water into the hole. Don't fill the holes in. Some suggest trimming the roots of the young leeks to make planting easy, but I prefer to twirl the plants round as I lower them into their holes so that the roots are in the bottom. Plant in rows 12 inches apart, with the plants 8 inches apart. Do not plant more closely as this hinders air movement

between the plants, which encourages orange leek rust on the leaves (and greatly weakens the plants). This method will give about 5 inches of white blanched leek. This can be increased by 'earthing-up', i.e. drawing soil around the leek stems as they grow. Soil can be prevented from getting into the leek by slipping the leaves and stem through a collar made from the cardboard insides of loo-rolls.

HARVEST   Autumn and through the winter. Like parsnips, it is said that leeks taste much better after a hard frost. Wonderful with a rich cheese sauce.

Lettuce & salad leaves

Just about anyone and everyone in the entire British Isles ought to grow their own lettuces, as well as some of the fantastic array of salad leaves available as seeds. The fragrance and taste of home-grown salads beats anything you can buy. Never, ever buy those lettuce seedlings that you see, usually in polystyrene blocks, in garden centres, for they are a waste of good money (one pack of eight costs more than three large lettuces from the farm shop). They really are a doddle to grow from seed. Lettuces can be grown in the ground, or in pots or tubs, and by sowing a few seeds every two to three weeks, you can easily provide excellent fresh salads throughout most of the year (from at least March to the end of October). My own first crops are grown in the cold greenhouse, but if you haven't got a greenhouse then try a sunlit window sill or porch. Winter crops of lettuce are a bit more tricky, for in our cool wet climate mildew can devastate them (see below).

SOWING/CARE Lettuce seeds are best sown in pots of good seed compost. I take two 4-inch diameter pots and sow two varieties of lettuce in each (see below), one pinch of seeds (no more than about 10–12) in each half of the pots. Cover lightly with compost, water, and put in a clear poly bag in the light (e.g. on a window sill). Every morning check them and as soon as the rounded seed-leaves appear, take the pots from the poly bags and grow on in the lightest place you have. When the seedlings are about 1 inch tall (but no more), transplant them. Soak the soil in the pots and tip them out. Separate the little lettuce seedlings carefully and plant them 3 inches apart in your pots, tubs, growbags or garden beds. Water well and, when the plants are touching, cut every other one and enjoy eating them young. In the meantime, the others will grow to the maximum size for flavour and texture.

Five varieties of lettuce growing in a fish box.

Lettuce seedlings planted three inches apart in a box.

For a crop that will stand until Christmas, sow in August and transplant to a container in a sheltered corner or cold greenhouse. For a crop that will be ready for cutting in the New Year, sow indoors in late September and transplant in a warm greenhouse (minimum temperature 7–8°C/45–48°F). The problem with the greenhouses of we amateurs is that they will have been used to grow tomatoes etc., and almost certainly the spores of mildew will be in the air. So I forego home-produced lettuces after Christmas, and clean and sterilise the greenhouse (using a greenhouse sulphur candle) in mid winter.

I grow all kinds of salad leaves, such as Lamb's Lettuce (hardy and good in the winter months), Rocket (lovely and peppery), and various mixes (such as Thompson and Morgan's Herby Salad, Niche Oriental Salad Leaves and Brown's Mesclun Mix, which are tasty mixes of leafy species), in shallow 8-inch pots. Sow the seeds thinly, a good pinch of 20–30 seeds, across the compost in the pot and cover lightly. When they are at a nice size (4 inch tall) I harvest about one third of a pot and mix that with my young lettuces, leaving two more cuttings in the pot. No supermarket can come anywhere near that in quality! Yet the cost of one meal for two is pennies. It just takes a few minutes in time and effort.

VARIETIES   The lettuce NOT to grow if you like flavour is Iceberg. Grow a mixture including soft butterhead and crisphead varieties; for visual impact, also grow a red/purple variety. Many writers praise loose-leaf lettuces, that don't form hearts and that can be picked over a long period. I personally find that in green varieties the flavour and fragrance is not as good as the hearting varieties. So try Clarion, Tom Thumb and Cassandra (butterheads), Little Gem (Little Gem Delight from D. T. Brown is outstanding) and Chartwell (Cos), and Lollo Rosso (a red loose-leaf with great flavour).

For salad leaves, French Mix, Oriental Salad Mix and Mesclun Mix (D. T. Brown) or Herby Salad Mix (Thompson & Morgan) are excellent. Try also Rocket, Lamb's Lettuce and Water Cress in containers.

Sow small amounts regularly for wonderful salads.

You can add all sorts of ingredients to your lovingly grown lettuce, and dandelions, nasturtiums and pansies are just some of the edible flowers that really do enliven a plate full of greenery! If a tortoise can eat it, so can you!

Onions, shallots and garlic

Onions from sets

Sets are immature bulbs that are planted in the ground in spring or autumn and are harvested as onions in late summer or late spring. They are much easier than growing from seeds, though bolting (producing a flower and not a large onion) is a problem, but one that is reduced if you buy more recent varieties.

PLANTING/CARE   Plant the sets 4–5 inches apart in rows 9 inches apart, so that the tips of the little bulbs just show at the surface. Don't just push them in; plant using a trowel or by making a shallow furrow with the corner of the rake. Check regularly to make sure that none have been pushed out by the lengthening roots (sometimes a problem in clay soils). I then put short canes in and around the onion bed and run a network of garden string between them, to keep cats and birds off the bed and provide support for the onion leaves. Keep the bed well weeded. You will have raked in some general fertiliser before planting; it may be worth giving a weak liquid feed when there are three or four leaves showing. Water well in dry weather, but not during the last month before harvest as this slows ripening.

In cold springs it may not be possible to put onion sets in the ground in March or April. Start them off in pots, inside, instead

HARVEST   Onions are ready for harvesting when the tops fall over. Leave them for a week or so and then loosen the roots gently with a fork. When the tops begin to wilt, carefully dig up the crop and put them to dry, in the sun, on trays or in shallow boxes. In the evening or if rain is forecast, take them indoors (a garden shed is ideal). Use onions that have produced a flower stalk or that have thick necks first, for they will not keep. When the rest have dried, either store them in strings or in a soft bag (the leg from a pair of tights is ideal!). Check weekly for any of the store that is 'going off'. Well-dried spring-sown onions will last well into the New Year. In contrast, autumn-sown onions will not keep long but provide a crop that can be used before that year's spring-sown are ready (May–July onwards).

VARIETIES   For the autumn (maincrop) harvest, plants sets out in April, varieties Centurian, Hercules or Setton. Red Baron is the recommended red variety of onion (although I have grown it twice and didn't have a great crop). For the spring crop from over-wintered onions, plant sets in September as above, varieties Radar or Senshyu Semi-Globe Yellow.

Onions from seed

Most folk do not grow from seeds, because sets are so much easier. However, keen gardeners often prefer seed to sets, especially when trying to grow big onions. Sow the seed in late January (those trying to grow huge onions sow on Boxing Day!) in modules or cell-trays or in a seed tray, indoors with a minimum temperature of 5°C/42°F. If sown in a seed tray, carefully transplant the seedlings into modules or cell-trays when they are still in the bent hair-clip shape, avoiding knocking off the remains of the black seed case. If you want big onions, transplant into 2-inch pots when their roots fill the module or cell, then later into 4-inch pots. Ideally the plants will be kept in a warm greenhouse (they need plenty of light as well as warmth) until ready to plant out in late April or early May, when the weather and soil have warmed up. Plant a minimum of 4 inches apart in rows 9 inches apart (a foot apart if you are trying to grow large onions). If you are trying to grow mega onions for the local show, or just to impress the neighbours, it is easier to purchase plants from Robinson's, the home of the Mammoth Onion at Forton. Harvest as for spring-planted sets.

VARIETIES   Bedfordshire Champion, an old but outstanding variety, Santaro F1 is a great new one; for giant onions try Lancashire's, Robinson's Mammoth Onion.

Spring onions

These are easy to grow in 10-inch plant pots. Although there are newer varieties on the market, White Lisbon is as good as any. Sow a good pinch on the surface of damp compost and cover lightly with more compost. Keep watered. By making sowings from February to May you can have spring onions for seven months of the year.

Shallots

PLANTING/CARE   Shallots are grown from sets, as onions, but instead of them growing larger they produce more sets of the same size. They have a more subtle flavour than onions, and are excellent pickled. Plant the sets in early March, 6 inches apart, and they will be ready for harvesting in August.

VARIETIES   Dutch Yellow and Giant Yellow are most often seen in the garden centres, but Pikant and Golden Gourmet have the edge for spring planting. In recent years we have seen the introduction of shallots that are said to be culinarily far superior to the old varieties. These varieties were developed in France, so growing them here in north-west England may be a bit of an experiment. Thus far I would recommend growing them in the lowland coastal plain, and giving them cloche protection through the winter. They are planted in late autumn and harvested the following summer. Try Jermor (raised in the Rhône valley) or Echalotte Griselle (though now 'French' has its origins in central Asia). Good crops in Lowton!

Garlic

In my youth, if you wanted to grow garlic then you planted cloves obtained from the upmarket veg shops, as few wanted to cook with it at the time and it was not widely available. The trouble was that they were cloves from much hotter climes, and Lancashire is somewhat different from Provence! Then garlic began to be grown in the Isle of Wight, and seed suppliers began to provide varieties such as Early Wight, Solent Wight and Purple Wight. Though fine for the far south of England, these varieties were not as successful hereabouts, so I was thrilled to find garlic specially grown from Ukraine stock (called Chesnok Wight) that likes cold (and, I hope, wet) weather. It is in the ground as I write and looks in tremendous form! So to grow garlic in our county, look for one of the newer varieties with origins in the colder parts of Europe.

PLANTING   Separate the cloves, discarding any tiny ones, and plant them in October or early November, so that the soil just covers them, 6 inches apart in rows 12 inches apart. You can also plant in spring, but early garlic produces best after suffering the frosts of winter.

HARVEST   When the leaves and stem have turned yellow (usually July), harvest and let them dry out in the sun. Home grown garlic is superb!

Parsnips, salsify & other non-brassica roots

Some people like parsnips, some don't. I love them roasted, my wife is not over keen, so I grow about a dozen using the method below. As for salsify and its close, black-skinned relative scorzonera, most people have never tasted them. Which is a pity, for they have a quite unusual and excellent flavour. The problem with these last two is that, when peeled, the white flesh turns brown in the air, and that can put people off (and is possibly why we don't see them in the shops). The problem is easily overcome by dropping peeled salsify or scorzonera into water into which a squeeze of lemon has been added, immediately after peeling. We both like salsify, so I grow about 40 of them for winter use, two per meal.

SOWING/CARE   With my clay soil, I use the 'crow-bar technique' for growing these. Using a crow bar, make cone-shaped holes about a foot deep, 8 inches apart in rows 12 inches apart. These I fill with a mix of sieved homemade compost (about 40%), sieved loam or mole hill (40%), and sharp sand (20%), adding a good handful of general fertiliser per bucket of the mix. Three or four seeds are put on the top of the filled cones, and they are covered by half an inch of the same mix. Water well. Sow parsnips in March, salsify/scorzonera in the second half of April. The latter germinate within a fortnight, but parsnip seedlings may take longer to emerge and better germination is guaranteed by using the wet kitchen roll technique (page 57). When the first true leaf (as distinct from the first strap-shaped seed leaves) begins to grow, remove all but the one strongest seedling at each point, and water after doing so. That's it – but remember to keep them weeded.

RECITE

Scorzonera or salsify gratin

I have modifed a River Cottage recipe that makes a lovely dish in its own right. Peel and slice plenty of roots (you need roughly 6oz per person) and cook them gently in a 50:50 mix of vegetable or chicken stock and white wine, just enough to cover them. They will take about ten to fifteen minutes – don't overcook. In the meantime, finely grate some top quality Lancashire cheese and mix, again 50:50, with fresh, white breadcrumbs. Drain the roots, with the cooking liquid going into another pan. Put this on the boil and reduce by half. Then add about half the volume of cream or low fat crème fraîche. Thicken this with either cornflour or a beurre manié (flour and butter mixed before cooking). Put the cooked roots into a shallow gratin dish, pour over the creamy sauce, and top with the cheese/breadcrumb mix. Brown in a hot oven and enjoy.

VARIETIES   Try the parsnip Gladiator; it's an F1 hybrid and excellent. Mammoth (or Sandwich) is a good salsify, Russian Giant a scorzonera.

HARVEST   Dig up as you wish to enjoy them between mid autumn and the end of winter. If hard frost is forecast, dig a few and store in a frost-free but not too hot place. Boiled and roasted is fine, but you could also try the following recipes, though there are many others available in books and online.

Salsify roots, simply served
with butter and parsley,
or you can try the recipe
shown on the left.

Spiced parsnip soup

*Fry or roast about 6 parsnips, chop and put into
pan with 1tsp cumin, ½tsp turmeric, 1 chopped
onion, a garlic clove, 3 plum tomatoes, chicken or
vegetable stock and seasoning. Boil for 10 mins
then liquidise. You can add ginger or a pinch of
cayenne pepper or chilli for more of a kick. Serve
with plain yoghurt or sour cream on the side and
fresh crusty bread.*

Parsnip crisps

*Scrub the parsnips clean then slice thinly with a mandolin
or the slicer on your cheese grater – aim for a diagonal
slice. Heat a wide pan and add a couple of glugs of olive or
vegetable oil. The oil will be hot enough when a tiny bit of
parsnip fizzes when you drop it in. Add your sliced parsnips.
Shake and toss the pan to keep the slices turning, trying to
keep them well spread out. Use a slotted spoon to help. You
can make these in batches if there are too many for one go.
The parsnip slices will caramelise, then crisp up. Keep them
moving so they don't over-brown. When cooked to your
satisfaction – crispy in places and caramelised in others –
move from pan to kitchen roll-dressed plate. Dab with more
kitchen roll to soak up excess oil, then liberally add sea salt
and freshly ground black pepper. Serve at once but be careful
as they will still be very hot! You can use this recipe for
scorzonera, salsify and beetroot too.*

Peas

Everyone knows garden or green peas, which can be bought frozen at the supermarket in splendid condition ... indeed in better condition than the 'fresh' peas from the market that need to be shelled. Better? Yes, because commercial growers have them shelled and frozen within a few hours of picking, and the ones that you might buy to be shelled at home would have been picked at least a day or two before they got to the shop. Some have argued that frozen peas are of such quality and low price that it is not worth growing your own garden peas, and the land could be used to grow something better. And if land is at a premium, I would agree and say grow mangetout or sugar snap peas instead. Ordinary garden peas may be cheap in the shops, but mangetout and sugar snaps are not, so it is worth growing these delicious vegetables yourself, and peas too if you have lots of space.

SOWING/CARE   Use the gutter method. Buy or otherwise acquire some lengths of plastic gutter and saw them into manageable lengths (about three feet). You need enough for the length of row you want to grow. Fill the gutters with a good seed compost and then sow the pea seeds 3 inches apart throughout the gutter (not just in a single line). Cover with an inch of compost and water well. After about 10 days the young pea shoots will emerge and, in another couple of weeks or so, the little plants will be about two inches tall. Then is the time to move them into the ground. Having raked some general fertiliser into the bed, scrape out a shallow trench into which the gutter will fit. Then water the gutters well and slide the young pea plants and compost from the gutters into the trench. Water again. Finally, erect some plastic pea netting along the row using canes for support.

VARIETIES   Hurst Green Shaft is an old, prolific and good tasting variety of garden pea that grows well throughout Lancashire and I wouldn't try any other. It can be sown in here from mid March to June, cropping from the end of June to very early September.

Mangetout/sugar snap are more or less one and the same thing (see below)and new varieties are excellent, such as Delikata, Sweet Delight, Sugar Ann and Kennedy, as are older ones such as Oregon Sugar Pod.

HARVEST   Put the kettle on, pick the peas and shell them if they are the garden variety, and cook them immediately or eat raw. Don't let garden peas get too big or they lose some of their tenderness and sweet flavour (the sugar is turned to starch). Pick mangetout/ sugar snap either when the pods are large but the peas have not developed (mangetout translates literally as 'eat all') or when the peas have developed to form sugar snaps, in which case trim top and bottom and pull away any 'strings', as you would do with runner/French beans. Both types freeze well, just blanch for one minute and drain throughly before bagging up.

Potatoes

South-west Lancashire and much of Cheshire are very lucky because the mossland produces great spuds. Some farmers even get a very early crop of new potatoes by growing in a polytunnel. So there is no need to try to grow all the potatoes needed by your family. However, everyone ought to grow some early new potatoes at least, for there are varieties not available in the shops that taste outstanding. And you don't need ground to grow them in.

A note about sweet potatoes: you may see sweet potato 'slips' and Mayan potato seed for sale, but growing this vegetable is generally not successful in Lancashire unless you live by the coast and have a warm polytunnel.

Garden pea seedlings, having been slipped into their bed from guttering, are watered. Those seedlings in the white gutter to the right are mangetout. They will be planted next.

Four seed potatoes were planted in this special bag. Using bags or large pots enables early crops to be grown in the greenhouse, or a few early potatoes when there is no space in the ground.

PLANTING/CARE   Buy seed potatoes as soon as they are available (usually late January or February), and plant singly in 12-inch pots or in threes or fours in larger tubs. You can buy special potato bags or 'planters'. Definitely *avoid like the plague* those planters advertised that come complete with seed potatoes, for the varieties offered are not necessarily the best tasting and often include maincrop, which we can buy cheaply here in the North West from the farmers who grew them. I plant up a couple of tubs in February and in early March keep them in the frost-free conservatory, and eat them in May or early June, about a month before the first outdoor plantings. For compost I use a mix of garden compost and loam/mole hill, adding a handful of a general fertiliser to each bucket of the mix. Half fill the tub, put in your seed potato(es), and cover so that the tub is three quarters full. Keep well watered – this is vitally important if growing potatoes in containers. When the plants are higher than the tub, fill up with compost.

Seed potatoes that are not used immediately should be put in the light for 'chitting', whereby you arrange the tubers in a shallow box (egg boxes are ideal), with the end with lots of 'eyes' (tiny buds) uppermost and put on a window sill. Shoots will grow from the eyes. Some writers have said that there is no advantage in chitting seed potatoes; I think they are wrong!

My grandfather *always* planted his new potatoes on Good Friday, ignoring the fact that Good Friday can occur from about 20 March to almost mid April. Don't be in a hurry, for a frost will kill green growth above ground level. Plant 4–5 inches deep at the beginning of April, in rows two feet apart and with the seed potatoes one foot apart in the rows. Keep an eye on the weather. If the potato plants are showing above ground and a frost is forecast, cover the shoots with newspaper, weighted down to stop it being blown away. When the plants are about 9 inches tall,

You really can't beat home-grown spuds! I reckon that new ones are best enjoyed simply with butter, salt and pepper, and sometimes you can add some of your home grown mint, roughly torn. Later in the season you can do just about anything with most varieties, but probably my favourite is proper home made chips, preferably with the skins left on.

you must 'earth them up'. Failure to do this will result in at least parts of the spuds being green, and the green is poisonous (never eat the leaves or round fruits of the potato plant). Draw soil up around the plants in the row so that the shoots stick out of a ridge and the forming potatoes are well buried. Some try to keep light away from the growing potatoes by using a black polythene sheet, though I have found in the clay soils of Lancashire this attracts slugs, which make holes in the spuds. Water well, especially in June, when the new potatoes should be growing quickly.

VARIETIES   If you have good soil, or for pots and tubs, try the old Arran Pilot; if you have clay soil, Duke of York, Sharpe's Express, Epicure and Casablanca are excellent. Go for flavour.

HARVESTING   Your outdoor-grown potatoes will be ready in July, indoor tubs 11–12 weeks after planting. It is said that new potatoes are ready when the flowers either fall off as buds or open. But why not have a careful look? Pull away the soil gently and look at the new potatoes. Ideally they should be the size of a hen's egg. Don't dig them all up at once. Take one plant at a time; dig the potatoes with a garden fork and make sure you take the titchy ones as well; go directly to the kitchen, wash your potatoes and immediately put into a pan of boiling water which has a bunch of mint added. When cooked, drain, then smother in melted butter and add a sprinkling of salt. Fabulous.

Spinach

The old Popeye cartoons, in which he bashed Bluto and terrified his girlfriend Olive Oyl, were produced in order to encourage children to eat green vegetables like spinach. When I was a boy and watching Popeye on television we never saw, let alone ate, spinach. Why? 'Slimy horrible stuff!' said my grandmother, disappearing into the kitchen. Yet it is easy to grow and, despite what the aged g-p said, it tastes splendid!

Spinach hates hot dry weather and in a drought seedlings will run to seed easily (i.e. produce flowers instead of lush leaves). So make sowings in late March–May for harvesting through the summer, and make another sowing in late August–early September for a back-end crop. Water well if the weather is dry.

SOWING/CARE   You can either sow thinly (at about 1-inch intervals) an inch deep in drills of well-raked soil, in rows a foot apart. Thin to 3 inches apart and then when the plants are touching remove every other plant.

HARVESTING   Eat cooked or raw within minutes of harvesting. You should pick the outer leaves from all your plants and enjoy them. The plant will then grow more leaves. In 2011 I had five large pickings from one row of 15 plants. Or alternatively you can sow 3–4 seeds in 3-inch pots or modules and, when they have germinated, discard all but the strongest one and, when the plant roots are touching the sides of the pots, plant out, 6–8 inches apart, either in the ground or containers.

VARIETIES   Sigmaleaf is the best of the older varieties but the newer F1 hybrids Zebu and Florana have the edge.

Splendid ways with spinach

One of the main things people do wrong with spinach is to immerse it in a pan full of water, overcook it, and then not season the resulting unappetising mush. It can of course be eaten raw and is a brilliant salad leaf, but if you want it cooked, steam it very briefly, until it is just wilted rather than annihilated. I love it quite simply, with butter, salt and pepper, but it also goes very well with cottage cheese, onion and nutmeg for a pasta or baked potato filling, or with garlic, mushrooms, parmesan and black pepper as a side dish.

RECIPE

Sweetcorn

If you like sweetcorn bought at the local market or farm shop then you will *simply love* home-grown sweetcorn, for it is far, far sweeter than the bought stuff. The reason is simple: as soon as a cob is cut off its parent plant it starts to turn the sugars that make it so sweet into starch. So, by the hour, sweetness declines. Put on the kettle. Go to your veg plot with a big pan. Cut the cobs and run as quickly as you can to the kitchen! In with the boiling water and onto the stove.

SOWING/CARE   Sweetcorn does not like cold wet weather, so sow two seeds in seed compost in 3-inch peat pots or cardboard loo-roll tubes in late April or early May and keep on a warm sunny window sill or in a heated propagator. Remove the weaker seedling and grow the stronger on until the beginning of June when the weather will be suitable for planting them out. Slowly get the plants acclimatised by putting them outside for a few hours around midday. Plant in a block, not in a row, 18 inches apart. This is so that pollination is enhanced; also tap the plants when the long pollen-producing tassels are hanging down. Sweetcorn likes moisture around its roots, so make sure that there is plenty of humus down there: rotted manure, garden compost etc. And it likes full sun, not shade.

Each plant will produce one or two cobs, so work out how many cobs you're likely to need (you can freeze them) and provide enough space to achieve this.

VARIETIES   Go for a new F1 hybrid. Thomson & Morgan have one called Northern Extra Sweet that produced well in our dreadful 2011 summer, while Brown's Swift and Wagtail are fabulous.

HARVESTING   When the tassels have just turned dark brown the cobs should be ripe, but check. Pull open the green sheaths surrounding the cob and squeeze two or three grains. If a watery liquid is produced, leave for another day or two. If a creamy liquid exudes, the cob is ripe – so into the pan with it, NOW!

If squeezing your corn to check if they are ready to harvest results in a doughy gunge, you are too late. Don't worry too much, though, for that is the quality of most shop-bought sweetcorn!

SOS – Save Our Seeds!

Provided that you keep your seeds well sealed up in their (usually) foil packet, and keep the packet in a sealed container in a cool, dry place, most will last for more than one season. Parsnip is an exception, for its seeds will usually not germinate after one year. So for vegetables where we need only a few plants – such as tomatoes, peppers, courgettes, aubergines – sow just a few and keep the rest of the seeds for next year. Packets of seeds of things like lettuce, cabbages and sprouts usually contain a lot, so sow pinches when you need to and store the rest. I have known some lettuce and cabbage varieties to be viable after five years, so there is no need to buy a new packet every year. I usually grow about six lettuce varieties, but in any one year have to buy only one or two new packets.

If you want to know if last year's seed is still viable, give some a quick soak and put them between sheets of wet kitchen tissue. Check daily and if none has germinated in a fortnight they are not. But you will be surprised how long some seeds can survive if looked after properly. You could keep some seeds from your own plants, but be aware, especially with the new F1 hybrids, that your seed will not produce the same variety. The ones that are worth saving are from French and runner beans, for the purchased packets of seeds are relatively expensive and have too many seeds for one season. So let a handful of pods ripen and, when the seeds are dry, pick them and store in envelopes with your other seeds.

Young, pampered seedlings that were grown either indoors or in a greenhouse need to be acclimatised to cooler temperatures, lower humidity and increased air movement for about two to three weeks before they are planted outdoors. This 'toughening up' process is known as hardening off and it helps prevent transplant shock. For more information about hardening off methods visit www.rhs.org.uk.

79

GREENHOUSE SPECIALS

...or how to beat our NW climate!

I CANNOT THINK OF ANY GARDENER I KNOW WHO, having a greenhouse, does not grow tomatoes, and most grow a cucumber plant as well. An increasing number are also trying to grow their own sweet peppers, chillies and aubergines. So because cultivation of these greenhouse crops is so similar, I will deal with them all together. I have also included courgettes and squashes here, and those big courgettes called marrows, even though they are mostly grown outside. The main problem with growing all these is that we have gluts, and either end up giving lots away or making chutney that spends years in the back of the cupboard before being thrown away! At the end of this section I will suggest alternatives.

Many gardening books talk of outdoor tomatoes and cucumbers, and that you may grow aubergines and peppers outside. However, I would not recommend growing any of these outdoors in Lancashire and its neighbouring counties, where our summers can be cool and wet. In 2010, 2011 and 2012 I tried outdoor tomatoes (two cherry varieties, Sweet Million and Cherry Falls) and my crop of ripe ones was poor because it was so late. In the

dreadful 2012 summer, outdoor tomatoes completely failed. So think 'greenhouse', or perhaps conservatory or sunny porch, and if you are going to buy a greenhouse, buy one a size bigger than you think you need!

The seeds of all these vegetables, with the exception of courgettes and squashes, are sown early, when frosts are still likely, so that heat is needed. Some gardeners avoid this problem by buying plants that are ready to be planted out in the cold greenhouse at the end of April or early May (NEVER buy them earlier, despite garden centres having tomato and pepper plants on sale in March). However, buying plants does reduce the choice of varieties unless you are member of a gardeners' association, where other members may offload their excess plants. For years I used warm window sills and put the pots in which I had sown seeds in a polybag close to a radiator. But if you can afford it, get a thermostatically-controlled propagator, then everything is under control.

Cucumber

Some folk say that it is either difficult or impossible to grow good tomatoes and cucumbers in the same small greenhouse: 'The indoor ones [cucumbers] are more difficult to grow well [compared with outdoor ones]' (Caroline Foley, *The Allotment Source Book*).

I have not found this to be the case in north-west England, however. In fact, with our generally cool climate – compared with the south-east – I find the opposite to be true, for cucumbers need a minimum temperature of about 16°C (61°F) to thrive and, save for the balmy coastal strip, only in the very warmest summers is this likely to be met from June to the end of August. So my advice is that you grow your cucumber in a greenhouse, with your tomatoes. I always grow my cucumber in a tub close to the door, which is kept open in warm weather.

Sow seeds in a propagator, one per 3-inch pot, in seed compost, in March or the first half of April, ideally at about 21°C (70°F) and then plant one into its tub at the door end of your row of tomatoes; most families need only the one cucumber plant, unless there is a cucumberaholic in the house, and I give any spares away – these are always well received because it is amazing how good a home-grown cucumber can be compared to a shop-bought one.

Train your cucumber up a cane by tying it in as it grows. Eventually it will out-grow its cane, so continue training it along a wire wherever you have space. I stretch wires over the door and then along the other side of the greenhouse. Water and feed with a high potash liquid tomato feed as you do the tomatoes.

VARIETIES   The cucumbers you see in the supermarkets are long, so long that most families cannot eat a full one, so many are sold cut in half. Forget the big cucumbers and go for little,

'all female' sweet ones. The F1 Emilie is my favourite, and in the dreadful summer of 2012 my one plant yielded nineteen 20cm (8 inch) long cucumbers over several weeks. Alternatives are Socrates and Superbel. Incidentally, if you like to put some of what you grow into your local autumn show, don't worry about length in cucumbers, for my little Emilie won the Red Card at our show a couple of years ago, thrashing some veritable giants!

HARVESTING   Cut the ripe cucumbers when they have reached maximum width, have a slight give when squeezed gently and give off a slight whiff of ripe cucumber.

Tomatoes

SOWING/CARE   I make two sowings, one in mid to late February and one in early April, to give me the six plants that provide us with more than enough tomatoes through summer and early autumn. At each sowing I sow one seed, a quarter of an inch deep, in each of six 3-inch pots of good seed compost. Usually all six germinate, which means that our gardeners' association gets some spares to sell on; but I keep the best three. After about three weeks I pot them on into 4-inch pots, planting them deeper, with the strap-shaped seed leaves just above the surface of the compost. The plants then grow extra roots from this small length of buried stem.

The three plants from the February sowing go into tubs in the greenhouse in the third week of April, those from the April sowing are tubbed about the end of May. I use my own compost mix. I don't use shallow growbags because the watering is more fiddly and blossom-end rot (where the end of the growing tomato rots through erratic watering) is a big risk. You could use the compost from growbags in big pots, two growbags to three or four large pots. The deeper type of growbags, known as 'planters', are far better but more expensive, though you can plant three tomatoes in one of them. At the same time, I put a long cane in place alongside each plant, and fix the canes to wires stretched the length of the greenhouse.

Check the plants daily and at first water if the surface of the compost is dry. As the plants grow it may be necessary to water daily; if growing in growbags you may have to water morning and evening in very warm weather. It is essential to feed the plants as you water them, using a high potash tomato liquid feed, following the manufacturer's instructions. Watering correctly comes with experience: make sure that the compost never dries out and that any excess water can drain away.

In hot weather (temperatures above 20°C, 70°F) keep the greenhouse door and any vents open; in cooler summer weather open them in the day and close them in the evening. If you let the humidity build up, mildew, blight and other fungal attacks might occur and kill the crop, so you need movements of fresh air through the greenhouse.

Pinch out any side shoots that try to develop in the axil between leaf and stem; also any shoots that develop at the tips of flowering shoots (often in the variety Shirley). As the plants grow, tie them

securely to their supporting cane, making a double turn around the cane and one round the stem. When the plants reach the greenhouse roof (they will have 6–8 trusses developing) pinch out the tip of the plants. When the tomatoes in the lowest truss have grown large, encourage them to ripen by cutting off all the leaves below and immediately above the truss so that the sun reaches them. You might also encourage ripening by hanging your family's bunch of bananas over the wire near the truss. The ripening bananas give off the gas ethylene, which hastens ripening in all fruits.

If trusses are very large they may break and you will lose part of your crop. To prevent this, cut off the outer flowers/tiny fruits and, using soft garden string, support the truss by tying its tip to either the cane or wire.

VARIETIES   My favourite normal-sized tomato is the F1 hybrid Shirley; it is thin skinned and tastes delicious (forget old commercial varieties like Ailsa Craig, Moneymaker and Alicante ... whichever you choose from the catalogue, go for top flavour). If you want to grow large beefsteak tomatoes, try (Super) Marmande or Country Taste. Most of us like cherry tomatoes (eat them from the plant or grill a truss per person with steak or lamb chops); Gardener's Delight is the usual choice, but the newer Favorita, Sweet Baby and Suncherry are even tastier.

HARVESTING   Pick and enjoy them as they ripen. When we get towards the middle of September, and the nights draw in and the temperature falls, ripening noticeably slows. Cut off all the leaves from your tomato plants to expose the fruits to the maximum amount of sunlight. If you have a huge greenhouse with the potential for growing lots of tomatoes, you can get a very early helping as follows. Cut the top of one plant after it has produced a couple of trusses; water it until the tomatoes have reached a reasonable size and then water every third day. The plant panics, thinks that the end is nigh, and rushes to ripen its small crop.

Don't just grow bog standard varieties of fruit and vegetables, experiment a little! As long as they are suitable for our north-western climate be brave and have a go ...

... these are just 3 of the beauties I grew and it was lovely to have so many different ...

... shapes, colours and flavours!

Aubergine

These glossy purple-black fruits are used in the Greek dish moussaka, and in other Mediterranean dishes such as ratatouille and tagines. They need a long growing season, so if you just need the odd plant it may be better buying seedlings in April. But perhaps the most useful small-fruit varieties are not available. Some varieties are said to be hardy enough to grow outside, but I would not risk it in Lancashire, especially away from the coastal plain.

SOWING/CARE   Sow as for tomatoes, one seed per 3-inch pot, in the second half of February, using a heated propagator. Never let the temperature fall below 16–17°C as you grow on the young plants, moving them into 5-inch pots in March. Then, move on into 10-inch pots, fixing two or three thin 'split' canes around the edge of the pot. As they grow tie the aubergine branches to these supports. Water whenever the surface of the compost is dry, adding high potash tomato fertiliser to the water.

Extraordinary aubergine

With very little effort (see the recipes below) these purple beauties can taste absolutely wonderful.

Roast the aubergine, peel then purée it with garlic and cumin, or with lemon juice, good olive oil and salt.

Slice it, rub with a peeled garlic clove and olive oil, and grill or BBQ both sides. Lay sliced tomatoes on top and grill again. Add salt and pepper to taste, place loaded aubergine slices on toast and eat at once!

RECIPE

VARIETIES   The aubergines that we see in the shops are large. You may grow such varieties, including Black Beauty, Listada de Gandia, Moneymaker and Early Long Purple, but you are unlikely to get more than six or seven fruits per plant. Instead, I would recommend varieties such as Baby Rosanna, Calliope (which has cream-streaked purple fruit)and Pot Black that produce lots of smaller 2–3 inch-long fruits over a long period (in the cool summer of 2011, from mid August to early October).

HARVESTING   Pick when the fruits are glossy purple-black.

Peppers & chillies

Sweet peppers and chilli peppers are so closely related that we will consider them together. Chilli fanatics can enjoy growing a wide range of varieties, each with its own heat level. This is measured by the Scoville Scale, named after Wilbur Scoville in the USA, and it is a measure of the amount of the chemical capsaicin in the chilli.

SOWING/CARE   Sow as for tomatoes, ideally in late winter (end of February) at 20°C; these plants require a long growing season, especially long-ripening chillies. I move them on into 5-inch pots in late March and then into 10-inch pots into the cold greenhouse in early May (or from mid April if the weather is likely to be hot). Put in split-cane supports and tie branches to these. When the plants are about 8 inches tall, encourage them to branch by nipping out the growing tip. With chillies you may nip out the tips of the first branches to encourage more fruits (sweet peppers need fewer branches because they produce fewer, larger fruits than chilli peppers). Keep them well watered, adding tomato fertiliser to the water.

VARIETIES   Excellent sweet pepper varieties include Ace, California Wonder, Topepo Rosso, Mohawk and Jumbo Sweet.

How hot do you want your chilli peppers? Meek & Mild is just that, Jalapeno Summer Heat is pretty hot, while Habanero is very hot. For the most macho gardener, however, nothing beats Naga Jolokia, which has over a million Scoville Heat Units. By gum, now that *is* hot!

HARVESTING   If you want to cut your sweet peppers green, do so when they are glossy green and well swollen (usually from early August). Or wait until they are a nice bright glossy red. Leave chillies in the warm greenhouse and as they age their heat increases. The heat continues to increase after you have picked them and as the chillies begin to dry out.

Marrows and courgettes

When I was a lad I loved growing marrows. I used to nurture them by feeding them heavily with tomato fertiliser every time I watered them, and when it came to September I used to bore my pals at school with the vital statistics of my biggest. My grandmother Ada, who lived with us and did all the cooking, humoured my efforts by stuffing the tasteless beasts with either minced sausage meat or minced beef, plus onions, and baking them. The family 'enjoyed' slices of this concoction with mashed spuds, liberally applying lots of tomato ketchup or HP sauce to give it some flavour.

SOWING/CARE   Sow the oval seeds on their flat sides. That is important, for it makes it easier for the oval seed leaves to push their way out of the potting compost or soil. I sow two

marrow/courgette seeds in a 3-inch pot of seed compost in a warm propagator in early March. I remove the weakest seedling and then plant the stronger one on to a 5-inch pot at the end of March. This is kept frost-free on the kitchen window sill before I plant it in a 14–16-inch tub in the greenhouse in late April. I then make a second similar sowing (with a sowing of squash) at the end of April, and a third sowing at the end of May. These are planted outside at the end of May (after the last frosts) and the end of June, respectively. Again, I prefer to grow these in large tubs, but they could also be planted in the ground. By making these three sowings, I cut courgettes from June through to the first frosts. Keep them well watered and feed with tomato fertiliser.

Marrows and squashes are grown in exactly the same way, other than don't allow a plant to have more than two marrows or three squashes otherwise they will be an embarrassingly small size. Feed well and, as they enlarge, arrange support below, such as a big piece of slate or a large flat board. And keep on feeding and watering, day in and day out.

VARIETIES   Go for F1 bush courgette varieties, such as Defender, Best of British or Midnight. If you want a yellow variety, try Floridor (the courgettes are round) or Parador. And if you want to grow a marrow, try the classic Long Green Bush or the more modern F1 Tiger Cross or Zebra Cross. Try Harrier or Hercules squashes.

HARVESTING   Cut courgettes when they are still on the small side, with flowers intact (stuffed and deep fried, the flowers are delicious). Then you will get up to 20 courgettes per plant and sometimes in excess of that. Of course, that may mean a good half dozen each week, and if there are only two of you that is a lot of courgettes, so you might want to look at the section on page 90–1 in respect of the excess.

As for marrows and squashes, harvest carefully the day before your local flower show, and the best of luck!

I grew a couple of marrow plants in 2010 with a view to winning the 'red card' at our local flower show, but my entry was dwarfed by another which looked like it had been fed on steroids! The two marrows that I grew with such patience went for chicken food. Chickens love marrow.

Courgettes are completely different, much more flavoursome and can be used in many Mediterranean dishes. The squash will keep well into the winter, and their flesh is delicious.

Boozy marrow

We once tried making marrow rum, and this is what we did if you fancy a go. Take a marrow and cut off the end with the stalk. Now scoop out all the seeds — if you are any good at growing marrows, you will need a very long spoon! Now fill the cavity with demerara sugar, put back the cut end and fix it in place with a couple of wooden toothpicks. Then slide the marrow, blunt end down, into either a narrow muslin bag or the leg of a lady's tights and suspend over a clean bowl in a dark place. The theory is that the demerara sugar and marrow juice ferment over the next few weeks, slowly drip down into the bowl and produce a hooch that tastes like rum and can get you severely blotto. That's the theory. Since then I have been lucky enough to visit several Caribbean islands and sampled their rum, and I know which I prefer!

Courgette cake

If you like carrot cake, try replacing the grated carrots with two good-sized courgettes, and adding cocoa powder and orange zest at the flour stage. Makes a deliciously moist sponge. Top, if desired, with mascarpone and chopped nuts, or cream cheese combined with orange juice, vanilla extract and icing sugar.

Here lurks a potentially huge marrow!

What to do with greenhouse gluts

Those of us who grow tomatoes, peppers, aubergines and courgettes often find that we have gluts: too much, ready all at once. Early in the season I have too many courgettes, at the end of the season far too many tomatoes and peppers. Eat as much as you can fresh then it's time to get creative! Just a few of my favourites follow, but it's very easy to find lots of ideas and recipes in your books and online.

Ratatouille

This is a classic Mediterranean vegetable dish which rather conveniently makes excellent use of the usual greenhouse glut vegetables. Don't worry about precise measurements (the continentals don't!) and if you don't have all the ingredients you can always buy what you need, ideally from your local farm shop.

So, first of all, put the ripe tomatoes in a bowl with boiling water for a couple of minutes and then remove the skins.

Chop some onions finely and put them in a large pan with a good glug of olive oil, frying gently until soft, but not brown. Then add some pulverised garlic (chop the cloves, sprinkle with coarse sea salt, and then crush to a paste with a big cook's knife) and cook gently for a few moments. Chop the peeled tomatoes, aubergines, peppers and courgettes (or whichever of these you have grown or fancy) coarsely and put in the pan. Add a smidgen of tomato purée. If the mix looks a little dry, add some water (or wine if you like). If you like the mix to have a little heat, add one or more chopped chillies or chilli flakes or pepper. Thus far, almost everything we have used we *might* have grown ourselves, but don't beat yourself up if you haven't – I don't grow chillies so I use dried chilli flakes.

Now for the herbs. We will have thyme and marjoram and parsley in the garden, and a pot with basil on the window sill. Put these in your mix together with some (but not too much) salt and freshly-ground black pepper, then simmer gently until cooked.

Now you can have a dollop of this with your Saturday steak or piece of gammon or, as in Mallorca, with your Friday fish. Pop in some chopped chorizo for a lunch dish, or have it alongside scrambled eggs on toast. Or, if you are vegetarian, just enjoy with some pasta and grated cheese (Mrs Kirkham's Lancashire, or a real Cheshire Cheshire, if you can get it).

Moroccan tagine

Using the ratatouille recipe as your base, just add a Moroccan tagine spice mix (you can make your own using ground cinnamon, saffron, ginger, turmeric, cumin, paprika and black pepper, or try a ready-prepared blend available in supermarkets or independent retailers), some lemon zest, chopped dates and a spoonful of honey.

When you have a really good glut there will be too much ratatouille or tagine to eat at one go, so after enjoying several meals with the various Med mixes, I put the rest in freezer bags and freeze it. We had 14 bags of the lovely stuff that we enjoyed through the winter in 2011! And a nice bonus is that research has indicated that cooking tomatoes actually increases the amount of health-giving antioxident lycopene. It does reduce the amount of vitamin C, though, so fresh is still best for that.

Ketchup

Ketchup is also easy to make and perfect for a tomato glut. Having put them in a bowl of boiling water for a few minutes, peel and finely chop your surplus red tomatoes and put them into a pan with a little olive oil. Add a little salt, and some black pepper, basil, marjoram and parsley. I also like to add a small quantity of marsala wine, or you can add a little good malt vinegar. Cook gently for five to ten minutes, until the tomatoes are very, very soft, then liquidise or mash. You can enjoy this hot or cold and it will keep in the fridge for two or three days; otherwise freeze the excess, or put it boiling hot into sterilised glass jars with sealing lids.

Any tomatoes that stubbornly remain green you can always turn into a tasty chutney – there are plenty of recipes around for this or you can just make one up!

Soup

Then there's good old soup. I have found that you can make almost anything you grow into a warming, nutritious concoction, and the leftovers can be frozen or stored in sterilised glass jars with sealing lids (make sure the soup is piping hot when you jar it, and that you put the lids on straight away).

Some less-often grown vegetables – but don't let that stop you!

Artichokes

There are two completely different sorts: Globe and Jerusalem. The Jerusalem is nothing to do with the biblical city, but comes from the Italian word 'girasole', meaning that its flowers follow the sun. In the former we eat part of the flower head, in the latter tubers that grow underground.

GLOBE   Globe artichokes are delicious, but they hate poorly drained clay soils. They do grow well on silt and loam, however, or sand where there is plenty of organic matter dug in. Having 'enjoyed' only clay soils in Lancashire, I have had at best moderate success with globe artichokes, but those of you who garden around Newton-le-Willows, Wirral, Formby, Southport

and Lytham St Anne's should have little difficulty raising a good crop. Try them in the herbaceous border if you don't have a large vegetable patch. Harvest when they are still closed globes – if you leave them too long they flower, which means they are then inedible, although it is almost worth allowing a couple to do this as they are amazing in bloom!

The usual form in which you will come across globe artichokes in the shops is marinated in oil and herbs, or part of a greek salad, often with olives and feta cheese. The whole globe can look a bit daunting so below is a short guide to its preparation and consumption.

Wash well in cold water, trim off the stem to make the base flat and remove some of the lower outer bracts. Next trim the thorns on the ends of the leaves (if there are any) with a pair of scissors or a sharp knife. The artichokes may be boiled or steamed for 45 minutes (make sure your steaming pan doesn't boil dry) in a pan with a tight-fitting lid. Drain and when cool enough to handle, serve with melted butter, hollandaise sauce or mayonnaise. Peel off a leaf, dip the base in your chosen sauce and nibble the soft edible parts of the leaf with your teeth. Discard the leaf and take another one. Eventually you get to the heart of the artichoke. Remove and dispose of the fuzzy part (the choke) and use a knife and fork to eat the heart, dipping it into the remainder of your sauce.

TIP & RECIPE

RECIPE

For luscious leaves . . .

Cook the green leaf as spinach, and steam the white stems and eat like asparagus, with plenty of butter and black pepper. Lovely! You can also simmer chard with chopped tomatoes (tinned will do if you don't have enough fresh), garlic, onions, chickpeas and herbs for a warm, satisfying accompaniment to a meal. Fry the stems with the onions in a little oil or butter, then add the rest of the ingredients, the leaves cut into ribbons. Simmer gently for at least half an hour, in a large lidded pan, season and serve.

JERUSALEM   Jerusalem artichokes are extremely easy to grow (plant some tubers in February or March, harvest in winter). They may be roasted, mashed (try them mashed with carrots and sweet potatoes), made into soup, fried and served in a white wine and cream sauce, simply boiled and buttered, or peeled and grated raw into a salad with a lemon dressing. Please be aware, however, that eating too many Jerusalem artichokes will usually result in an unsavoury amount of wind!

Chard

Swiss and Ruby Chard are forms of leaf beet; the latter has beautiful red stems and a poor flavour, the former is white-stemmed and delicious. Most people never come across them because they rarely, if ever, appear in the shops or markets. You don't need a lot of plants. Sow three or four seeds at stations a foot apart and, when the plants are growing well, thin out to one per station. Keep watered and, when the outer leaves are large, with half- to one-inch wide stems, pull them away from the plants carefully. The plants will continue to grow more leaves over a long period, provided you keep them watered.

The first year that I raised Swiss chard I grew a row of 24 plants. What a glut! Neighbours and friends couldn't keep up with them and they don't freeze well. I even sent a team from BBC's Look North West home loaded down with bags of the stuff! Half a dozen plants is more than enough for the average family.

Celeriac & celery

I have thrice tried to grow celeriac and celery, and neither was successful due to my soil. Yet in West Lancashire you can see acres of peaty mossland covered with perfect self-blanching celery plants, and some farm shops sell the celeriac that they have grown. So I'm afraid I've admitted defeat and buy the few I need from farm shops in the west of the county.

If you do have soil that will grow celeriac and celery (and lucky you!) I would go for an F1 variety such as Ilona (celeriac) and the self-blanching Octavius (an AGM celery). Sow the seeds in March or April, putting five or six seeds in modules or small pots. When the first true leaves appear, thin out to one plant per pot. Grow on in a frost-free environment and in late spring (after all risk of frost has passed) plant out – celery plants 8 inches apart in a block and not in rows, celeriac 12 inches apart. Keep well watered and, until they are well established and growing strongly, cover with fleece. The close spacing, in a block, of self-blanching celery helps with the blanching, but to help the outer plants be well blanched also, put a low barrier to light around (e.g. some boarding). To encourage the growth of the celeriac root, remove the outer leaves when their bases split as the root swells. Harvest celeriac from September through to New Year. Harvest celery through the autumn.

Super soup

Celeriac makes very good soup – particularly so with cubes of blue cheese melted in after blending. It can also be roasted, mashed or is delicious raw. To make a salad, cut off the outer skin, slice into match sticks (julienne) and enjoy with sliced apples, walnuts, lemon juice, mayonnaise and seasoning to taste.

RECIPE

RECIPE

Chicory doo dah

This is a delicious Dutch recipe. Wash chicory and remove outer layers. Simmer in water for 25 minutes, then strain. Meanwhile, make a cheese sauce: melt 1tbsp butter, mix in 1tbsp plain flour, add ½pt milk and keep stirring. As the sauce thickens, add 3tbsp of the grated cheese of your choice. Take each chicory stalk and wrap it in a slice of ham. Place in a baking dish, smother with the cheese sauce, top with breadcrumbs and more grated cheese and bake until golden brown. Or you can eat chicory raw, in a salad with, for example, fennel, orange and kohlrabi, or with pear, apple and blue cheese.

Chicory

I tried growing the forcing type (also known as the Whitloof or Belgian chicory), which produces white chicons when forced, in my youth and haven't since, though I have two friends who have, successfully. Get a modern variety, such as Zoom F1, and sow in late May or June in a good, well-drained soil. As the seedlings grow, thin to 8 inches apart. This is one crop that must not be overwatered, for the root must be enouraged to go deep in search of moisture, and the longer the root the better. The latter point explains why it is easier to grow in deep sandy or silty soils, than in clay soils. In November cut off the top foliage and dig up the roots, trimming them to a length of about 12 inches (cut from the bottom of the root – don't damage the crown!) and storing them in a box of moist sharp sand in a frost-free shed. Then, about a month from when you want some blanched chicons, take some roots and plant them in a deep pot, with the crowns just showing. Keep them in the pitch dark at a minimum temperature of 10ºC. Break off, don't cut off, the chicons, for more smaller ones will grow until the root has exhausted its food stores.

Mushrooms

These are easy to grow from kits and today a wide range of types are available. However, the cost of the kits can be high if you take into account the time they take and the quantity of mushrooms produced. But gardeners with children or grandchildren ought to try growing a kit at least once, for education and fun. Myself, I prefer to pick my own field mushrooms.

Water cress

Most people think of water cress as growing in large waterlogged beds fed by the calcium-rich chalk streams of Hampshire, but it is dead easy to grow at home. Go to the

supermarket and buy a bag of water cress, preferably English (I have seen water cress grown in the USA on sale here, which is as ecologically illogical as asparagus from Peru and French beans from Kenya). Get an old washing-up bowl and make a few small holes in the sides close to the bottom. Half fill with compost (John Innes No. 2 is ideal) and give it a good soak. Now cut the water cress shoots just below a leaf node (where the roots will appear) and plant a few in your bowl. They may wilt at first, but within a week or so they should have roots and be growing nicely. Keep the compost wet and in a few weeks you can harvest some lovely peppery water cress. Planted in late October, you will have a good crop for Christmas.

If you involve children in your gardening, put a few shoots into a jam jar of water with only the inch at the tip sticking out. After a few days they will notice roots growing, and all from leaf nodes. Get them to plant the watercress carefully (roots are fragile) into a pot of wet compost, and eventually they will be able to make their own water cress sandwiches.

Two funny vegetables

I always think it's funny that melon seeds are listed among vegetables in seed catalogues and rhubarb invariably finds itself in books on how to grow vegetables. Yet we eat fresh melon as a fruit, and we cook rhubarb in puddings! Can you imagine tripe and rhubarb, or hot pot and melon? However, I am assured that melons are in the same family as gourds, and although botanically they are fruits (in the same way as tomatoes, peppers and pumpkins are fruits), they are grown and harvested in the same manner as vegetables. Rhubarb, meanwhile, is a close relative of garden sorrel, so is technically a vegetable!

Melons

SOWING/CARE   Sow in 3-inch pots of potting compost in April, making sure that the flat oval seeds are placed flat on their sides so that the seed leaves can emerge easily from the soil. Put the pots in a propagator or in a polybag on a window sill and keep at temperatures no lower than 18°C/64°F. When germinated, keep them in the warmth (minimum 15°C) until the end of May. Then slowly harden them off before planting them in 12-inch pots which are then placed in either a frame or cold greenhouse. When four or five leaves have grown, pinch out the tip of the plant to encourage branching. In a frame the branches will trail over the ground, but in a greenhouse it is easier to train the branches up a vertical support (canes and wires). Water whenever the compost surface is dry, adding tomato fertiliser to the water.

Melons have separate male and female flowers, and the latter are easy to identify from the embryo melon (small bulge) immediately behind the yellow flower. Make sure that bees can get into the frame or greenhouse to carry out pollination, especially on warm days when lots of flowers are open. Note that in cold weather or very early in the season, the embryo melons may not develop and may instead fall off the plant. Eventually some of the embryo melons should begin to swell, after successful pollination. Then nip out the growing point of the sideshoot two leaves beyond the potential melon.

VARIETY   Sweetheart is the most reliable, and very delicious. Ogden is a good alternative.

HARVESTING   A well-looked after melon plant living in a greenhouse in a long warm summer will produce up to five ripe melons, but in a cold grey summer there may be only one small melon per plant or even none at all! Sweetheart melons produce a sweet aroma when ripe, and the fruit feels soft close to the stem. If in doubt, give them another few days, as there is nothing so disappointing as finding your home-grown melon has the texture that is typical of the supermarket melon – as soft as a cricket ball!

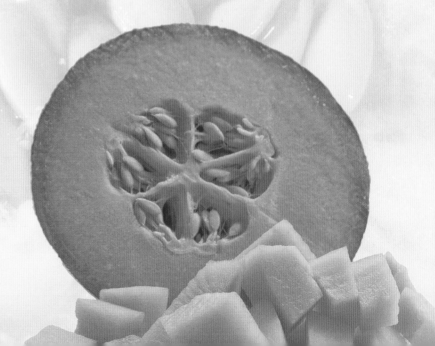

Rhubarb

Though it is possible to buy rhubarb seed, the usual way of acquiring new plants is by buying bits of crown, or scrounging them from friends. Plant the crowns three feet apart in a compost-rich soil, with the buds on top of the crown just at the surface, and water well. Take no harvest in the first year. Then, in late January of the second year, cover at least one of your crowns with an upturned container that will keep out the light (e.g. a deep bucket or old dustbin). This will give you lovely, delicate pink forced rhubarb in late March and April. From May, expose the forced crowns to sunlight, feed with a general fertiliser and take no other crop; the leaves will then build up the energy needed for the following year's crop. The other crowns will produce more solid, unforced rhubarb. Pull the younger shoots up to the end of July but never pull more than half the sticks or leave fewer than four per crown. After the last picking, again feed with a general fertiliser.

Rhubarb is a perennial. In October the leaves will die, so put them on the compost heap. During the late winter put a few forkfuls of garden compost or rotted manure and a sprinkling of general fertiliser around the crowns. After about five years the rhubarb plants will start to produce several flower spikes and weaker sticks, indicating that it is time for the crowns to be divided. Do this in winter by digging up the big crowns and cutting them into pieces, each with several eyes. Plant one or more of these, ideally in a fresh part of the garden, and give the rest away.

Life's end for a rhubarb plant is when the crown rots and the only sticks are thin and spindly. It's then time to dig up and put the old crown in the recycling bin (NOT the compost heap), and buy some more.

Beware: rhubarb leaves are poisonous, do not let children put bits in their mouths.

VARIETIES   I grow Timperley Early, which is excellent when forced, and Champagne Early, a lovely red and sweet variety.

Protect sprouting rhubarb from cats with wire netting.

HERBS

Wonderful flavours, easy to grow

'WHEN I WERE A LAD TIMES WERE 'ARD,' and most Lancashire families had access to only a very limited range of herbs: mint with lamb, sage with the Christmas stuffing, and that was about it. Then, in the late 1960s, dried mixed herbs became available in the first supermarkets, and we all began to be a bit more adventurous. I discovered that these greatly enhanced the flavour of many dishes, from roast chicken to steak and kidney pie, from tomato dishes to good old Lancashire hot pot. So I decided to have a go at growing my own. There really is nothing like fresh herbs in home cooking, and what's more, they are easy to grow.

Some species of herb hate standing in wet soil – notably French tarragon, bay, oregano and marjoram (very close relations), rosemary, sage and thyme – so in the sodden ground of our region I find it best to grow a good range of these in containers. Some (like horseradish and the mints) can become rampant and spread like weeds if left in the ground, so they are best grown in containers anyway. The lovely basil will not thrive in our northern climate other than in long hot summers, so that is better grown in pots and raised in the greenhouse, conservatory

or on a sunny window sill. You can mix herbs in large containers, but beware of having very tall and very short together as the tall may crowd out the short. Similarly, keep mints to themselves.

Don't use a peat or similar organic (coir, local authority recycled) compost for growing your herbs as this may get waterlogged in heavy rain. Instead use John Innes No. 1 or 2 potting compost and mix in a couple of handfuls of sharp sand or grit into every bucketful of compost to increase drainage. Check your herb containers regularly and in summer droughts keep them watered.

A herb by herb guide

Not all herbs will succeed in the climate of the North West but that still leaves plenty that will. The following are all ones I'd recommended for you to grow for culinary use.

Basil

An annual. Basil is too tender to grow outside here, other than in exceptional summers, so grow in pots in a warm sunny place (greenhouse, window sill). Sow a sprinkling of seeds in pots of well drained compost every three weeks from April to July, and harvest the leaves when the plants are 6–10 inches tall.

USES   Essential in tomato salads (scatter ripped leaves over slices of tomato after they have been doused in a good salad dressing, or layer with slices of beef tomatoes and mozzarella). Vital in all dishes with cooked tomatoes and tomato sauces, e.g. ratatouille, pizza, bolognese. Whizz up with olive oil, pine nuts, garlic, grated Parmesan and salt and pepper to make a deliciously fresh pesto.

Bay

A perennial (if you protect it from cold). This is a bush that cannot withstand extremely cold winter weather (my two were killed by the 2010/11 winter, having survived the pretty cold 2009/10 winter). So buy a young plant from the garden centre in spring and plant it in a 5-inch pot. When the roots have filled that pot, move it into a 10-inch pot and finally a 12-inch pot. Keep in a sunny corner and then, when the first very hard frosts are forecast, bring into the greenhouse or conservatory, or even indoors, making sure you keep it well (but not over) watered.

USES   Take the dark green, tough leaves and use in rich stews etc. as part of a bouquet garni. They contribute a bitter tang to a sweet stew and add excellent flavour to homemade stock and soups, or as flavoursome decoration to a homemade pâté. They are just added for flavour, though, and are too tough to eat. They also dry well (hang twigs of them upside down in a darkish place indoors) and as long as they are completely dried out (very brittle and crispy) you can put the leaves into jars and use them all year.

Chervil

An annual. This is one to grow in the ground by sowing a few seeds in rich soil, then thinning to one plant. It grows up to ten feet tall, with a big spread, in ideal conditions. But keep well watered, as in dry hot weather it can quickly run to seed and then die.

USES   Its distinctive liquorice flavour enhances all sorts of things, including mixed salads (add the leaves at the last moment), the sauce in chicken and mushroom pie, and all manner of fish dishes.

A young bay tree

Coriander

An annual that dislikes cool cloudy conditions, so here grow it in a pot in the greenhouse or on a window sill. Sow a few seeds in a 6-inch plant pot every three or four weeks from April to June, and do not allow the compost to dry out. Use leaves while they are young.

USES   The leaves are great in salads, but the possibilities are almost endless – see below. If you look after the plants they will flower and may produce the seeds that are essential in curries.

Dill

An annual. Sow from seeds or buy small plants and grow on in deep pots or well-drained garden soil in full sun. Use the feathery leaves fresh or, for winter use, dry in late summer. It grows up to three feet tall, and plants should be one foot apart.

USES   The seeds can be used to flavour white wine or sherry vinegar for use in salad dressings. Use the leaves to flavour fish dishes (e.g. poached salmon and gravadlax).

Fennel

A hardy perennial. In autumn the 3–5 foot tall shoots and leaves die back; cut them off at ground level and new shoots will appear the following spring. You can grow fennel from seed, or buy a couple of plants from the garden centre. Plant in a corner of the vegetable plot, in full sun.

Coriander combos

Everyone knows that carrot and coriander go wonderfully together, but why stop there? Try:

❖ *coriander with pineapple* ❖
❖ *replacing basil in pesto recipes (with cashews)* ❖
❖ *added to guacamole for a different flavour* ❖
❖ *with peas in place of mint* ❖

RECIPE IDEAS

USES   Lay fronds under sea bass or salmon steaks that are to be baked in the oven. Fabulous! If you like fish, you must grow fennel.

French tarragon

A perennial that doesn't like hard winter weather. So buy a plant or two from the garden centre in spring and plant in well drained compost. Flavour is best when grown in full sun in hot weather.

USES   I love this herb, it is so fragrant and infinitely better fresh than dried, so well worth growing yourself. Put a few sprigs into white wine vinegar and olive oil for dressings, or just chop roughly into a mixed leaf salad for a nice aniseedy flavour. It is also gorgeous in creamy sauces with chicken, pork or fish, maybe with wholegrain mustard, and I like it chopped and folded into scrambled eggs at the last minute. Just use the leaves though, avoid the stems which are rather chewy.

Horseradish

A perennial. Buy some roots and grow in deep containers. The kitchen needs pieces of root, so in autumn take the plants from their containers. Bury most of the thick roots, cut into sections, in a box of sand and store in a cool place, taking a piece or two out when needed. Plant some of the roots back into containers for next year's crop.

USES   Peel and grate the root and mix with a little cream or mayonnaise to make horseradish sauce. This is great with roast beef and with any smoked fish.

Marjoram and oregano

Both are members of the *Origanum* genus and have a pungent almost spicy aroma and flavour, so you can grow one or the other, or both if you wish. Though perennials, here in the North

Where would the ever popular Spaghetti Bolognese be without marjoram and oregano?

West it is best to grow them afresh every year. You can grow from seeds, or buy plants from the garden centre. They like poor soil, so I grow them in a tub of John Innes No. 1 (which has fewer fertilisers in it than Nos 2 and 3).

USES   Many Italian and Greek dishes just wouldn't be right without these two herbs. They are both excellent with tomatoes (especially in a Caprese salad), added to leafy salads, and with nice fat olives and feta cheese.

Mint

A herbaceous perennial that will grow almost anywhere. It loves Lancashire's wet clay soils, but it can become an invasive weed if not kept under control. So grow in a big deep pot of garden soil and keep well watered. In autumn the aerial parts will die back. In spring empty the pot, fill it with fresh soil, and plant sections of 'root' from last year's remains just below the surface.

There are a surprising number of different types of mint.:

- Straight 'mint' is the essential ingredient of mint sauce to eat with lamb.

- Spearmint leaves can be chopped with other herbs to add flavour to barbecued meats, or bruised and added to summer drinks.

- Chocolate mint leaves add a great flavour to summer puddings and ice cream.

- Apple mint shoots add an excellent flavour to cider vinegar; put a few shoots in a bottle of the vinegar.

- Moroccan mint is used for the authentic sweet tea drink.

Parsley

Here in Lancashire, most of us are used to having curly parsley in Friday's cod with parsley sauce, for a sprig or two may usually be had from the fish stalls in our wonderful markets. In recent years, however, TV celebrity chefs have prattled on about using flat-leaf parsley. Personally, I prefer the curly and that is what I grow, but the choice is yours. Both types of parsley are hardy biennials that like rich soil, and three or four plants will provide enough for most families from summer through to the following spring. In spring, soak some seeds in lukewarm water overnight and then sow them in a pot of good compost. Put the pot in a poly bag, seal the bag and keep on a sunny window sill until the seedlings emerge. Prick them out into 3-inch pots of the same compost and then, when well grown, plant out in the vegetable plot.

USES   In parsley sauce, as part of a salad, added to homemade dressings (lemon or orange juice, olive oil, salt, parsley, stirred together and used immediately) or as part of a bouquet garni. The flat-leaf variety makes a delicious addition to a poached egg on toast. Butter the toast, adorn with a generous handful of parsley, place your egg on top and finish with lots of freshly ground black pepper.

Rosemary

A perennial shrub that hates wet soil. So buy a plant or two from the garden centre in spring and pot on into a 10-inch pot by itself or as centre of a tub of mixed herbs. In September take a few cuttings (they root easily in a compost containing plenty of sand or grit) and keep them away from frost. Rosemary will survive most Lancashire winters, though I lost mine in 2010/11. The cuttings will replace any losses outside. If you don't need the new plants, give them away.

Rosemary cutting after 1 year.

USES   The leaves can be a bit sharp, so when using with other herbs on barbecued meat, chop them finely. Fabulous with roast lamb: put some sprigs under the lamb, or make slits in the skin and slip in bits of rosemary and garlic. Add to homemade gravy with a teaspoon of blackcurrant jam for a rich, dark sauce. It can also be part of a bouquet garni.

Sage

A perennial. Buy a plant from the garden centre in spring and grow it in a 10–12-inch pot containing a well-drained compost. I love growing this, not only because it is a herb I really like the flavour of, but because it produces such attractive flowers, which encourage our precious bees.

USES   Wonderful in our traditional stuffing of course, but also in creamy sauces with pork or poultry. It is quite pungent and holds its flavour well during cooking, so you need to use it relatively sparingly.

The purple sage blossom is loved by bees and other insects, and the plant in bloom is really very pretty.

Thyme

A perennial that is exceedingly hardy, but doesn't like waterlogged soil. Buy plants from the garden centre in spring and grow on in 10-inch pots or tubs of mixed herbs. Of the several varieties, two must be grown for their different uses.

Common thyme is an essential component of a bouquet garni for use in stews and casseroles. It goes brilliantly with chicken and lamb, and with game too, maybe with a good slug of port!

Lemon thyme, with its attractive variagated green and yellow leaves, imparts a lovely lemony flavour, which is quite different from lemon juice, and is particularly good in fish and chicken dishes, whether creamy or tomatoey.

Thyme in full flower – beautiful as well as delicious, and the flowers are edible, making a wonderfully fragrant and decorative addition to salads.

How to make a bouquet garni

A bouquet garni is simply a collection of herbs, tied together with string so that after cooking the casserole, soup etc. the tough stalks can easily be removed. Cut sprigs (or big bunches if you want plenty of herby ooomph!) of thyme, marjoram or oregano, parsley, rosemary and two or three bay leaves and tie them firmly together before sinking them into the dish before cooking. I sometimes add a sprig of chervil when cooking the breasts of chicken or pheasant in a creamy sauce. A real bouquet garni is miles better than those dry tea-bag things sold by supermarkets; it is a major reason why you should grow herbs!

FRUIT

fabulous colour and taste

FRUIT IS EXPENSIVE TO BUY, even at pick-your-own farms, though at least the fruit that you do pick yourself will be as fresh as grow-your-own, provided you use it as soon as you get home. I live only a couple of miles from the biggest pick-your-own farm in Lancashire, and when my own produce is not enough to see us through the winter, or for making the umpteen jars of jam that all the family scrounge from me (I love making it and love moaning when they ask for yet another jar!), I head for the farm.

With the exception, in my opinion, of strawberries, all soft fruits freeze very well. So too do damsons, and I de-stone large quantities with a cherry-stoner and pack them in pie-sized portions, then freeze them, ready for encasing in pastry in the depths of winter when you really need that kind of comfort food.

You can freeze tree fruits like apples, but they do eat freezer space. I cook windfall and damaged apples, either in chunks for pies and crumbles, or in more soft, purée form for apple sauce to go with pork and whatever else you fancy.

Of course, fruit can be used in many ways. Things like blueberries, strawberries and raspberries, and peaches and nectarines, are best eaten fresh. Excess raspberries and blackberries (together with its relations such as tayberries and loganberries), freeze well, as do blackcurrants and gooseberries, to make delicious winter puddings. Redcurrants and whitecurrants are mainly used fresh; mixed with other soft fruits they make a fabulous breakfast fruit to go with cereals, while redcurrant jelly is wonderful with roast chicken, turkey and pheasant. It is also worth collecting some crab apples and making crab apple jelly; it is lovely with lamb and pork dishes.

Jams? Damson, strawberry, raspberry, blackcurrant, gooseberry, plum, greengage? They are all well worth making. When you run out of the marmalade that you made using Seville oranges last January, don't buy the rubbish stuff for sale in supermarkets. Use the slightly tart gooseberry jam instead. Fresh (homemade if you're really good!) bread with a helping of your own jam makes a great light lunch or something to nibble on at four o'clock with a cup of tea.

You can't beat a good homemade jam sandwich, whatever flavour of jam you make!

Apples and pears

Many Lancastrians who buy apple and/or pear trees from their local garden centre end up being disappointed with their growth and crops. The reason is that garden centre proprietors have a tendency to buy in varieties that are popularly sold by supermarkets, such as Golden 'Delicious', Cox's Orange Pippin, Braeburn and Granny Smith. The problem is that these are NOT good varieties to grow in the North West! For Lancashire and the rest of northern England, you need to grow varieties that are much hardier, and, as luck would have it, they are often better tasting.

The second thing to remember when it comes to growing apples and pears is that, when you pick them, they may not be fully ripe and ready to eat. In fact, most will *not* be ripe and ready to eat, and they need to be stored in a cool, dark place until the time is right. This may seem strange, for we are told that apples and pears should be picked when, if they are lifted, the fruit stalk separates easily from the tree branch. That *is* true, but it does not mean that they are ripe. Let me give an example.

I long thought that it was impossible to grow a succulent pear here, believing that, if a late frost didn't get the flowers, then the fruits wouldn't ripen in our coolish wet summer and early autumn. This idea seemed to be confirmed when, having joined the committee of Newton-le-Willows Gardeners' Association, I was involved in the autumn show. I looked at the dish of Conference pears that had taken the first place 'red card'. They seemed perfect, but hard. When the show ended I bought that dish of pears and took them home. Rock hard. I put them in the fruit bowl, intending to poach them in white wine and honey, but I forgot about them. A month later I refound them. They were now soft and delicious … and ripe!

Tips for top tipples!

And then there are the tinctures … the little drinks that warm the cockles of your heart on a cold winter's evening. Sloe gin is traditional, but try damson gin instead. Or plum or cherry brandy. Or try soaking the fruits in vodka instead of gin or brandy. If you put the fruits plus some sugar in the appropriate spirit in late summer, the unctuous liquid will be ready for Christmas. In the dark of my wine cellar are old glass toffee jars and a gallon whisky bottle, scrounged years ago from the corner shop and pub, each holding two litres of spirit plus fruit and sugar.

Both apples and pears are worth growing, even in a flower border. At blossom time they are beautiful and then, as their fruits develop, they become fascinating and full of promise.

The varieties I cover below all grow well in Lancashire. Note that each variety of apple belongs to one of the pollination groups A to E, and that pollination is better if you have two or three different varieties in either the same pollination group (e.g. all in group B) or in adjacent groups (e.g. in groups B or C, or in groups A and B). But don't worry too much; if you grow your produce on an allotment or in a garden surrounded by lots more, bees will bring pollen in from all around. Apples will not pollinate pears and vice versa.

But first a note on root stocks and pruning, for there are several root stocks to which the variety of fruit that you want may be grafted. For smallish northern gardens and allotments I would recommend: for apple, either M26 or 106 root stocks – M27 is the most dwarf root stock, but is not recommended for northern areas; for pear, buy grafted on Quince A.

For all plums, gages, damsons etc. buy grafted on St Julian A root stock. Avoid trees grafted on Pixie root stock as this needs warmer conditions (and top quality soil ... not clay!) and here in the North West plums grafted on Pixie will tend to be stunted, especially away from the coast or in the hills.

There are many ways to grow your tree fruit: as bushes, in fans, as 'step-over' trees, as cordons etc. Follow the advice given in a good book, and here I would recommend *The Fruit Expert* by Dr D. G. Hessayon. I would also recommend any newcomer to vegetable growing to buy his companion volume *The Vegetable and Herb Expert* (see also reference in Further Reading, page 128).

Eating or dessert apples

DISCOVERY   The earliest, ready for picking from mid August. Eat immediately or by mid September. Lovely flavour. Pollination group B. James Grieve is a great alternative, juicy, crisp and fresh with an excellent flavour. Either is a MUST.

EGREMONT RUSSET   Some do not like the thickish, slightly furry-textured skin of russets, but for many others this is a highly prized apple, with a sweet nutty taste. Pick in the second half of September; ready to eat October–December. I also cook with it; delicious. Pollination group A.

LORD LAMBOURNE   A lovely sweet fruit, in aroma and taste, that will produce large crops. Pick in the second half of September; ready to eat October to mid November. Pollination group A.

ASHMEAD'S KERNEL   A 300 year old variety, I recommend this for its great flavour; but it is one for the lowland and coastal plain, and not one to grow in the hills of East Lancashire, Cheshire or Lakeland. Pick about the middle of October; ready to eat December–February. Pollination group A.

DUKE OF DEVONSHIRE   Raised in 1835 at Holker Hall in Furness (now administered as part of Cumbria), this truly Lancashire apple is very sweet with a touch of sharpness. A lovely apple. Pick October; ready to eat Christmas on into March. Pollination group B.

KESWICK CODLING   Also useful for cooking, the first of this variety was found growing at Gleaston Castle in Furness, which is part of the Palatine County of Lancaster, and later it was taken into a nursery at Keswick, hence its name. It has a lovely sharp, juicy flavour. Pick September; ready to eat from picking up to the end of October. Pollination group B.

Cooking or culinary apples

I first grew the following three varieties in my Fulwood (Preston) garden in 1959, and I still do grow them. They are a good trio for our county.

BRAMLEY'S SEEDLING   Perhaps the most famous cooking apple, the Bramley is what is know as a triploid (it has an extra set of chromosomes), so that it cannot pollinate other apples. To get the best out of it, grow with at least a couple of other varieties. It crops heavily in Lancashire but, unless you thin out the crop a little, it tends to produce good crops every other year. A lovely cooker. Pick October; ripe for cooking November– March. Pollination group B.

LANE'S PRINCE ALBERT   Gives a good crop of fine cookers every year. Pick late September–October and use from then until they are all gone. Pollination group C.

LORD DERBY   Lovely green-skinned, well-flavoured cooker, and if I could have only one cooker, this would be it. Very hardy. Pick October; ripe for cooking from then to Christmas. Pollination group D (so grow close to a group C variety).

And don't forget the crab apple, here being blitzed for crab apple jelly.

It really is worth restricting the crop on any apple tree. By allowing only one apple to grow from each flowering spot (where there will have been up to six flowers), you will get one large delicious apple, instead of two or three small bullets. Thin at the end of June, for there is a natural thinning out in that month.

A lovely pair of Bramleys, ready for the perfect apple pie or crumble, or if you are lucky enough to get a glut, stew and jar 'em to preserve!

GOLDEN SPIRE   A nineteenth-century Lancashire apple that produces yellow-skinned fruits of excellent flavour. Pick October; ripe for cooking from picking time to the end of November. Pollination group A.

LADIES FINGER OF LANCASTER   This is a Lancashire variety dating to the early 1800s which has fallen out of fashion; yet it is well worth growing. Pick October; ripe for cooking November–December. Pollination group C.

SCOTCH BRIDGET   My best pal, the late Alan Storey, who had a lovely medieval strip garden at Penwortham, near Preston, up until his early death had a collection of old Lancashire apples. 'Surely it is a Scottish, not Lancashire, apple?' I said. 'Actually, it's a very hardy, delicious cooker and it was popular in both Scotland and Lancashire until the Second World War,' he replied. Try it. Pick October; ripe for cooking from then to Christmas. Pollination group B.

Pears

If you only grow one variety, make it the Conference, as it will produce good pears in the north west of England and it is self-fertile; other varieties are not and you will need to grow at least two.

CONFERENCE   If you are going to grow pears, this is the essential one. The fruits are long and green, with good flavour. Pick September; ready to eat October–November. Pollination group C; this is self fertile, so can pollinate itself as well as others.

JARGONELLE   A very old variety, dating back to the time of James I, this is the one to grow here in the north if you *must* grow a second pear. It has a fine flavour and is very hardy, but is not a great keeper. Pick August; ready to eat August–September. Pollination group C, so will be pollinated by Conference.

WILLIAM'S BON CHRÉTIEN   An eighteenth-century pear that is hardy, though it dislikes heavy rainfall and waterlogged ground, so could be best grown near the coast in Lancashire rather than inland, and definitely not on clay. In hot summers you can eat this one straight from the tree. Pick September; ready to eat September. Pollination group C.

Plums, damsons and gages

The main problem with these is that they flower early and so a late frost can devastate the chance of a good crop. 2010, 2011 and 2012 illustrate this perfectly. In 2010 we had lots of late frosts and the crop was poor (the damson crop that makes the Lythe Valley so famous completely failed, and my own damson tree produced only 14 fruits). In 2011 we enjoyed one of the warmest Aprils on record and the crop was phenomenal (my small tree produced 42lbs). In 2012, however, we had a warm March, fairly cool April and the crop was only 8lbs, all on the lowest sheltered branches. But usually you will get some crop, making it well worth growing one or two of these closely related fruits. All those listed here are self-fertile, so you can grow one by itself.

Glorious greengages

Some people make the mistake of thinking that these are merely unripe plums, or that they are sour. Nothing could be further from the truth! They are considered by many to be the sweetest, most flavoursome of all the varieties and are amazing just eaten fresh from the tree. If you have a glut, they make wonderful jam, and equally good pie or crumble filling.

HERMAN   A very hardy plum bred in Sweden in 1972, which can be eaten fresh or cooked.

OPAL   Outstanding flavour makes this a great dessert plum. Needs plenty of sunshine, so one for coastal areas here in the North West.

VICTORIA   The plum to grow if you want only one variety; can be eaten fresh from the tree, cooked in pies and puddings or made into jam.

SHROPSHIRE PRUNE   This is the perfect damson for small gardens and allotments. The alternative is Merryweather, but this grows into a more straggly tree (I know; I have one!).

GREENGAGE   This very old variety is still worth growing, though cropping can be irregular (good crops some year, poor in others).

DENNISTON'S SUPERB   An American variety of gage that is outstanding both in taste and crop reliability.

PRUNING TIPS

Damsons, gages and plums: whereas trees like apples and pears are mainly pruned in autumn or winter, <u>always</u> prune plums etc, if you must, in the growing season (June–July)

How to prune

Refer to a good book when you come to pruning your fruit bushes and trees (Hessayon's *Fruit Expert* is excellent, but if you have ornamental trees and bushes that need pruning, Brickell and Joyce's *RHS Pruning & Training* is outstanding). Do not prune at all, and crop yields will fall; prune badly, and you could lose one or more year's crop altogether. However, whenever you come to pruning a twig or branch, always look at the bud immediately below the cut you make, for that bud will generate new growth in the direction that it points.

Generally prune above outward-pointing buds, so that they will grow out away from other shoots or branches, and so that the centre of the bush or tree will be open (this is sometimes referred to as pruning to get a goblet effect). And prune out any shoots that try to grow inwards through the centre of a bush or tree.

Young gooseberries and blueberries, for instance, require a slightly different approach. Their branches may trail close to the ground so that, when laden, their fruit are on the soil. In these, look at the buds and choose one that points upwards. Prune there, and the new shoot will grow up, away from the ground.

Generally, prune to an outfacing bud, so that the resulting growth will be upwards and outwards.

Cut

Apricots, nectarines and peaches

Writers who garden in the South and Midlands often refer to hardy varieties of these lovely stone fruits, but here in and around Lancashire they are best grown either on the coast, against a south-facing, white-painted wall, or in a greenhouse. Elsewhere and you will get no crop in many years. Go for old, well-proven varieties.

Apricot

MOOR PARK   This 250 year old variety has great flavour and good fertility.

Nectarine

LORD NAPIER   Good cropper; great flavour.

Peach

PEREGRINE   The best, by far.

Cherries

There are two sorts of cherry: sweet (that can be eaten straight from the tree) and culinary (that need cooking). The two recommended here are self-fertile; others are not and need another for pollination.

STELLA   A Canadian sweet variety that tastes superb and crops well. It needs plenty of sunlight.

MORELLO   A very old culinary cherry that will grow in heavy shade, including against a north-facing fence or wall.

Figs

The variety Brown Turkey is the one to grow here in north-west England. Grow it in a big pot or tub (up to 30 inches diameter); water well, but do not over-feed with fertiliser. After leaf fall, either wrap in fleece or take into a cold greenhouse or shed until spring. I didn't do this in 2010–11 and that hard winter killed my fig tree. Figs straight from the tree on a late summer or early autumn morning are a great treat.

Soft fruit

Soft fruit is expensive to buy, yet easy to grow, including in containers. Beware that most plants have a limited life span, for example: strawberries three years; blackcurrants and gooseberries around ten years. The reason for this is that they are susceptible to viruses that greatly reduce cropping.

Blackberries

Related to our native bramble, some are thornless, making pruning, tying in and picking easier. This category also includes hybrids that are well worth growing.

VARIETIES   Go for the newer ones, such as Apache (thornless with sweet fruit), Chesapeake (thorned, but with big luscious fruits), Kotata (thorned, good fruits, and disease resistant), Loch Ness (thornless, good fruit), Boysenberry (a hybrid, thornless, large fruit, good on sandy soils), Loganberry (hybrid, thornless, for cooking), Tayberry Buckingham (hybrid, thornless, large fruits).

Blueberries

These need a very acid soil, so are best grown in containers with ericaceous compost and watered with rain water (from a water butt). My two blueberries are growing in our old bath, sunk into the ground. For best fruit set, grow at least two varieties. There are lots to choose from. Bluecrop, Herbert and Northland (the latter a small shrub) are excellent. Eat the fruits, picked that morning, with your breakfast cereal. Can't beat 'em!

Blackcurrant

Go for the Scottish varieties, Ben Connon, Ben Lomond and/or Ben Sarek.

Redcurrant

The varieties Rovada and Rotet not only have great red berries but are disease resistant.

Whitecurrant

Choose from two varieties: Versailles Blanche or White Grape. The latter has the best flavour, but the first can withstand bad weather and has more disease resistance.

Gooseberry

Gooseberries are fairly easy to grow, though a torment to pick due to the thorns – wear some substantial gloves if you want to avoid injury is my advice! Many varieties are susceptible to American gooseberry mildew; this can be rampant in our cool, damp climate. Invicta (a green gooseberry) has good resistance and our own Lancashire Lad (my grandfather grew this in Bolton in the 1920s) has some. Fruits of Lancashire Lad can be left on the bush until they turn red and can be eaten without cooking. You could also try a pair of mildew-resistant varieties from Finland, Hinnonmaki Red and Hinnonmaki Green. However, if you want the best flavour you should grow Leveller if you have good soil, or Whinham's Industry if you are on a heavy clay soil.

PRUNING TIPS

Blackcurrants and blackberries flower on the previous year's wood, so in pruning you want to remove older branches and encourage these new growths every year. Redcurrants, whitecurrants and gooseberries flower on older branches, so pruning is vital in the first two or three years to produce a nice bush with branches spaced at regular intervals around an open centre. Thereafter, pruning can be quite light. In blueberries, simply cut out lower branches that will trail on the ground when bearing fruit.

Beware of the saw-fly. Daily, in late spring and early sumer, examine all the leaves and at the first sign of any leaves being devoured, leaving the spiky midrib, spray with insecticide or squash every saw-fly larva.

Grapes

In some parts of the British Isles it is possible to grow good grapes out of doors (and there are some vineyards in southern England producing outstanding wines). But not here, save for the most fabulous hot summer(!). What you usually get from outdoor grapes here are small, acidic ball-bearings. So, growing grapes means in a greenhouse or conservatory. For years I grew Black Hamburg and, provided I thinned out the grapes on each bunch, I got some big juicy fruits. However, the grandchildren didn't like the seeds; and neither did we. R.V. Roger Ltd recommends Crimson Seedless, their 2011/12 catalogue declaring: 'Unsurpassed for flavour, this red seedless variety needs the protection of a greenhouse (and even a little heat in spring in colder areas), but is the finest dessert grape we offer'. Need I say more?

Raspberries

There are two main types; summer raspberries and autumn raspberries. In the first, the fruits are borne on canes that grew from the ground the summer of the previous year, and in the latter the fruits are borne on canes that grew from the ground the summer just gone (i.e. in 2012, the summer raspberries were picked from canes that grew in 2011, and the autumn fruits from canes that grew in 2012). All canes that have fruited in summer are cut down immediately afterwards, to give next year's canes more light; all canes that flowered in autumn are cut down the following February.

SUMMER-FRUITING   I recommend either Glen Lyon (lots of fruit with excellent flavour) or Malling Admiral (great flavour); the latter is ready for picking a little later than the first and if you have the space, grow both.

AUTUMN-FRUITING   Autumn Bliss is the one to go for as it will fruit right to the first frosts. Though the autumn raspberries produce less fruit than the summer ones, they are lovely, fresh with breakfast cereal.

Strawberries

First, avoid those strawberry hanging baskets if you live in north-west England, for the plants seem not to be able to withstand the battering by the winds we get up here. Grow them in the ground (change the bed every four years) or in containers (I use fish boxes). Every year the plants will produce 'runners'; cut them off plants in their first summer but peg them down in pots of compost to provide new plants in the following year.

There is a somewhat bewildering range of varieties available. Currently I grow:

MAE AND GARIGUETTE   Very early strawberry varieties producing ripe fruits in May in the greenhouse.

HONEOYE AND CHRISTINE   Varieties that will produce early, fine fruits throughout June in a warm year.

HAPIL AND MALWINA   Slightly later, fruiting to the middle of July.

CALYPSO   Each plant produces a few fruits throughout from late June to September; a planter or box with six plants is good for two people.

The most popular commercial variety is Elsanta and many who grow only a few plants choose that one; for your garden the variety Mae is far better because of its finer flavour.

Eat 'em fresh!

Raspberries and strawberries grown at home are, provided you have chosen varieties for taste, too good for turning into jam or putting in pies and puddings. For that, go to the pick-your-own farm and jam or pie fruits from there!

TIP

CONCLUSION

SO THERE YOU HAVE IT, the fruit and vegetables to grow within the boundaries of old Lancashire. Believe me, what you grow yourself, provided things are picked and eaten at the right time, are far better than what you can buy (with occasional exceptions such as pick-your-own farms and some farm shops). But ultimately, nothing can beat the huge pleasure and satisfaction you get from actually growing the stuff yourself.

I get such a kick from taking a seed or infant plant, creating the right conditions for it to grow, nurturing it, harvesting and eating the end result of all my hard work. If I have inspired you to have a go, to believe that you can succeed, whatever space you have to grow in, I will be a very happy man. The guidance contained within this book is designed to give you the best chance of success by showing how to work with what you have, and what not to attempt to grow. I wish someone had given me the same advice about 50 years ago, it would certainly have saved me a lot of experimentation, time and failed crops! That said, there is a satisfaction in trying something and making it work, so never be afraid to test a gardening theory. You might well make a wonderful new discovery!

14 TOP TIPS FOR . . .

1. Make soil condition your main concern, and to this end, once you have double-dug your plot, have a no-tread regime. You can do this with raised beds, or you can do it by having beds that are narrow enough to be sown, weeded, watered and harvested from the paths. Then earthworms will do all the digging, provided that you feed them and the soil.

2. You must add as much humus to the soil as you can. Never, ever throw away peelings from veg, or the cores of apples, or used tea bags, or coffee grounds, or cardboard boxes. Put them on the compost heap or in compost bins with weeds, old annual flowers etc. from the garden. Tear up the cardboard, soak it, and mix it with your plant waste. If, like me, you have lots of prunings from things like buddleias, hydrangeas and roses etc., buy a shredder and compost them. In autumn, gather leaves to make leaf mould. If you have some riding stables or a dairy farm nearby, scrounge manure and add that to your compost bins. And every year put at least couple of inches (5cm) depth of compost on your veg beds and around your fruit trees and bushes.

3. Keep the hoe sharp and handy to win the weed war. A survey in 2012 found that a high proportion of new allotment holders quit within a couple of years because they found weeding hard. It is really only hard if you let the weeds take over.

4. Don't treat statistics on seed packets about how far veg plants should be spaced as though written in stone. Get more in and, as they grow, thin out and enjoy the thinnings.

5. Don't grow more than you can eat (an example is cabbage). Sow and grow a few every fortnight (e.g. lettuce) or month (e.g. French beans, beetroot) so that you are harvesting over a long period.

6. Remember, GYO is about flavour, not size or prize-winning at the local show! Buy seeds and plants that will guarantee greatness on the plate.

7. Veg loses its flavour after picking, so pick just or cut before you prepare a meal and get things like sweetcorn and asparagus into the boiling water seconds after cutting.

8. Be careful when you buy new fruit trees and bushes, as varieties on sale are often those that are most popular in supermarkets, such as the strawberry Elsanta (that has a good shelf-life), the apple Cox's Orange Pippin and Golden Delicious, and the pear Doyenne du Comice.

. . . GYO IN LANCASHIRE

Retailers selling them here in the north probably do not grow their own fruit! Instead, look for varieties that have the best flavour, and that have been developed here or been proven to grow well here in northern Britain.

9. Most of us think of blackcurrant bushes and apple trees, so that if we have only a small plot we may have room for only two bushes or trees. Instead, think of cordons or minarets. I have six cordon apples, of different varieties, in the space that two dwarf bushes would take. Cane fruits (raspberries, blackberries) and cordons are the best way to hide an unsightly wooden fence.

10. Unless you have a huge plot, don't bother growing maincrop potatoes and carrots, and perhaps even things like winter cabbages, which are grown in abundance and are inexpensive from farms on our mosslands. Just before Christmas 2012, 25kg bags of Nadine (the best potato for roasting) and Désirée (for chipping and mashing) cost £6–7 each, and Savoy cabbages less than a pound. Peanuts!

11. Don't get led astray with your timings for sowing and planting out tender vegetables by the displays at some retail outlets. For instance, I have seen tomato and melon plants for sale in March, which here in Lancashire may as well be described as late winter, at least a month too early unless you have a heated greenhouse.

12. If you have no greenhouse, but have somewhere to put one, buy one. Even better, perhaps, buy a polytunnel where you can grow all your veg sheltered from our often too cool and wet climate. A standard ten-by-six (10' × 6'/3m × 2m) greenhouse is big enough to raise lots of veg and flower seedlings through early spring, and then to grow plenty of tomatoes, aubergines, peppers and the odd melon through summer and autumn.

13. Consider carefully before you use chemical sprays and things like metaldehyde slug pellets. Fine mesh netting, which lasts for years if you look after it, will keep things like white butterflies off your brassicas, and carrot root fly from your carrots. These nasty chemicals can kill other, beneficial wildlife. I would greatly miss my hedgehogs on a warm summer evening, munching slugs and snails, as we sip a glass in the gloaming.

14. Enjoy! Join your local gardening society/association and the Royal Horticultural Society.

REFERENCES & FURTHER READING

1. D. G. Hessayon, *The Fruit Expert* and *The Vegetable and Herb Expert* should be on every GYO gardener's bookcase.

2. Caroline Foley, *The Allotment Source Book* and *The Allotment Handbook* are a mine of information on GYO.

3. Every year I obtain the following catalogues, not only so that I can order seeds, fruit bushes etc., but as a reference:

   D. T. Brown: 0845 371 0531 www.dtbrownseeds.co.uk

   Dobies: 0844 701 7625 www.dobies.co.uk

   Robinsons: 01524 791 210 www.mammothonion.co.uk

   Suttons Seeds: 0844 922 0606 www.suttons.co.uk

   Thompson & Morgan: 0844 573 1818 www.thompson-morgan.com

4. For fruit trees, bushes and plants I recommend R. V. Roger Ltd who have their nurseries in the north, but on the wrong side of the Pennines at Pickering! Their list is vast and includes useful notes on Lancashire, and provides other northern and hardy varieties.